PRAISE FOR BUSINESS GR

"Small business owners need to reconnect to what inspired them to start their business. Business Growth Levers will help you to step back and refocus on the important issues. Without technical jargon, this is a clearly written guide that any business owner can relate to and determine how to get to where they want to be. More than creating a more profitable business, it's about what you can learn to become a successful business owner and to improve virtually everything you do."

Marshall Goldsmith
2 million-selling author of the *New York Times* bestsellers, *MOJO* and *What Got You Here Won't Get You There*

"Business Growth Levers reconnects you to the dream you had of owning and running your own business but also takes you forward, into the future, where your business is achieving its full potential.
Ray and Clara have clearly walked this path and provide practical tips to help you accomplish more than you imagined."

Marcia Wieder
CEO/Founder, Dream University

"A truly invaluable gold mine of crucial information and highly effective strategies to aid in the growth of small business, Business Growth Levers offers the key to unlocking your business' unlimited potential. With their remarkable level of combined experience in virtually every facet of the business world, Ray and Clara Noble have written what I consider to be one of the most important business books of the year; if every business owner read and applied the strategies in these pages, the economy would be rocketing upward."

Ivan Misner, Ph.D.
NY Times Bestselling Author and Founder of BNI®

"What a brilliant idea! A list of the top 100 reasons a business may not be growing and what to do about it. In my experience businesses that are not growing suffer from a number of problems and don't know where to start. Read this book is where you start! Every issue has top tips and approaches for bringing about change in that area. It's tempting to read the ones you think apply to you, but my advice read the whole book cover to cover. You'll find additional areas you need to work on and what you need to avoid or develop for the future."

Mark Rhodes
Speaker, Mentor and Author of *Think Your Way to Success: How to Develop a Winning Mindset and Achieve Amazing Results* and *How to Talk to Absolutely Anyone: Confident Communication in Every Situation*

"Ray and Clara have done their homework, and present solid information that business owners can use to improve their dream business. There are very important yet basic fundamentals here that are often overlooked because the entrepreneur is buried in his perceived busy-ness."

Bob Nicoll
Chief Paradigm Shifter and author of *Remember the Ice*

BUSINESS GROWTH LEVERS

100 Challenges You Can Turn Into Opportunities!

Ray Noble and Clara Noble

Copyright © 2014 Ray Noble and Clara Noble
This book is a revised and updated version of Stunted Growth by the same authors

All rights reserved.
No part of this publication may be reproduced, stored or transmitted in any form or means without prior written permission of the authors.

While the authors have used their best efforts in writing this book, its contents reflect their knowledge and experience and they cannot be rendered liable for any results arising from interpretation or implementation.
Any Internet Web Sites offered as citations or resources may change or disappear between the time it is written and when it is read.

ISBN-10: 1495955214
ISBN-13: 978-1495955211

ACKNOWLEDGEMENTS

This book is the result of my personal 30 year journey as an auditor, CFO, business owner, coach and consultant working in various countries with a variety of companies with such different cultures as the UK, Saudi Arabia, Portugal, Switzerland and the US.

I've been fortunate to have a partner in most of this journey who I met in 1982 while working for Deloitte's, who became my wife in 1985, and since 2000 has been my business partner and co-visionary.

Her passion for work, even at the times when our professional paths had gone separate ways, has been a constant inspiration and our sharing of ideas and learning has supported both our careers.

I would also like to express my deepest appreciation to all the Mentors, Clients and Colleagues that have contributed each in different ways to help me to become the professional and the person that I am today.

To finish I have to mention my father who left school at 14 but was a great student of life. He taught me to listen to the customer, but then do the math. He used to say: *"Be a really good Supplier and you will find plenty of good Clients."*

Ray Noble

This book is the first step to the materialization of Ray's vision for the Mentoring side of our business.

I'm passionate, creative, restless and 'bossy' while he is calm, easy going and more analytical.
It has been a perfect match and we have accomplished together more than each could ever have done individually, with love and happiness as a bonus!

I would also like to express my deepest appreciation to all the people that have touched our lives and contributed to our joy and success.

Finally a tribute to my Mum who has raised me with two important beliefs:
First that I could accomplish anything I set my mind to do if I worked intelligently and persisted enough.
Second that I should always support others and only compete against myself.

These have been the pillars of my life.

Clara Noble

PREAMBULE

Who This Book Is For

This book is for **YOU** if you are an entrepreneur or small/medium business owner who has once had a vision and has dedicated a significant amount of time, effort and money towards making that vision become reality.

You have lived through the Creativity and Survival stages, having managed to materialize your dream and got through the first 18-24 months when about 30% of the new ventures fail.

Your company may have grown to anything between 5 and 50 million dollars and 10-100 staff depending on the area/type of the business. You have seen lots of victories along the way but you have also been through a lot of hardship.

Your business may be making a moderate profit but it has become harder and harder to keep it growing and it is draining your energy and perhaps taking a toll on your health and personal life.

Perhaps your company is already in the red due to the economy and overall market conditions. You may feel overwhelmed and fear that your life's dream may turn into your worst nightmare…

This book is also for you if you started a company in the last couple of years and you have not yet been able to quite make it profitable, but have clients and a firm belief in your product or service and its ability to make a positive impact in the world.

Finally this book is for all business owners who want to focus on solutions instead of problems and who want to take their business to the next level.

How To Use This Book

This book is about Growth and overcoming challenges that stop a business from achieving its potential. This is something that is not easily assessed by an outsider without serious investigation. YOU as the owner are in the best position to know what the goals are and what needs to be done to get to where you want to be.

However, sometimes being so wrapped up in the daily running of the business you become part of the problem, you lose the objectivity to be able to clearly identify what is holding things back. You can't see the forest because of the trees, it happens to all of us at times.

Business Growth Levers has been written to stimulate thought about various aspects of doing business and pinpoint areas for improvement so that in depth study can then be made. If used productively, it will provide many topics for reflexing or brainstorming with your team, if you have one.

Business Growth Levers will bring an increased awareness of the way your business is operating at this point in time and help you to find solutions you can start implementing right now to improve results.

Although everyone in an organization has a unique perspective of how things are few, if any, see the whole picture. You may come to the conclusion that the support of a Coach would save precious time and money by expediting the identification and implementation of the steps that will make your business thrive.

Read this book as the beginning of your journey to improved results. We challenge you to apply the ideas and guarantee you will see results! The extent of the results will be proportionate to your actions and your commitment to see them through.

You can make that quantum leap that will give you more financial ease and freedom while bringing increased satisfaction to your Staff and Customers. **It's YOUR call!**

CONTENTS

	Introduction	1
1	**Vision and Mission**	3
	01 Getting a Clear Vision	4
	02 Establishing a Set of Values	5
	03 Common Goal	7
	04 Conviction	8
	05 Too Grandiose or Not Ambitious Enough	10
	06 Lack of Strategy	11
2	**You**	14
	07 Knowing Where You Are	15
	08 Mindset	16
	09 Overcoming Fear	18
	10 Being a Better Leader	20
	11 Being a Better Listener	22
	12 Being a Better Speaker	23
	13 Being a Better Negotiator	25
	14 Being a Better Problem Solver	27
	15 Being a Better Manager	29
	16 Coping Better with Stress	31
	17 Dealing with Change	33
	18 What if You were Abducted by an Alien?	34
	19 Poor Health	36
	20 Loneliness	38
	21 Do You Know Where You Want to Go?	40
3	**Business Plans**	43
	22 Not having a Plan	43
	23 Unclear or Incomplete Planning	45
	24 Over Planning	47
	25 Contingencies Not Studied	48

	26 Integration	50
	27 Buy-In from Partners/Staff	52
	28 Reality Check	53
	29 Reviews and Updates	55
	30 Putting it Into Action	57
4	**Product and Marketing Strategy**	60
	31 Create First and Sell Later	60
	32 Lack of Research	62
	33 Knowing Your Competition	64
	34 Knowing Why You are Different	66
	35 Building a Brand	68
	36 Believing in the Power of Marketing	69
	37 Inconsistent Message or Unrealistic Marketing Plan	71
	38 Wrong Positioning and/or Pricing	73
	39 Too Much Competition	75
	40 Don't Know Your Customers	76
5	**Sales**	80
	41 Systematized Sales Structure	81
	42 Prospect Qualification	83
	43 Knowing How to Deal with Sales Objections	85
	44 Wrong Perspective on Closing	87
	45 Over Focus on New Customers	89
	46 Over Dependent on 1 or 2 Customers	91
	47 Customer Service	92
	48 Over Focus on Getting Orders	94
	49 Inadequate Sales Compensation Plan	96
	50 Insufficient Motivation	98
6	**Organization's Structure**	102
	51 Best Structure for the Business	102
	52 Flexibility	104
	53 Policies and Procedures	107

	54 Outsourcing Enough	109
	55 Outsourcing Too Much	111
7	**Organization's Culture**	114
	56 Repairing a Damaged Culture	114
	57 Making it about 'Us'	116
	58 Increase Quality	118
	59 Productive Meetings	120
	60 Resistance to Change	121
8	**Human Capital**	125
	61 Recruiting the Right People	125
	62 Lack of Orientation (Onboarding)	127
	63 Improving Training and Development	129
	64 Improving Communication	131
	65 No Career Planning	133
	66 Improving Performance	135
	67 Performance Reviews	137
	68 Improving Salary and Benefits Packages	138
	69 High Staff Turnover	141
	70 Lack of Good Staff	143
	71 Improving Leadership	145
	72 Improving Team-Work	146
9	**Finance**	150
	73 Accountant's Competence Level	150
	74 Improving Internal Controls	152
	75 Financial Plan/Budget	154
	76 Accounting Deficiencies	156
	77 Inadequate Analysis	157
	78 Looking Beyond the Numbers	159
	79 Finding the Right KPIs	161
	80 Confusion between Profit and Cash Flow	163
	81 Lack of Capital	164

	82 Badly Structured Funding	166
	83 Not Enough Cash	167
	84 Poor Credit Control	169
	85 Forecasting Cash Needs	171
10	**Purchasing/Supply Chain/Procurement**	174
	86 Leveraging Purchasing	174
	87 Improving Relationships with Suppliers	176
	88 Not Enough Suppliers	177
	89 Improving Inventory Management	179
	90 Reducing Waste and Inefficiency	181
11	**IT**	185
	91 Overcoming Fear of IT	185
	92 Lack of Solutions	187
	93 Improving Implementation	189
	94 Lack of Training	190
	95 Information Overload	192
	96 Evaluating the ROI	194
12	**Miscellaneous**	197
	97 Finding the Right Partners	197
	98 Succession	199
	99 Innovation	200
	100 Showing Gratitude	202
	101 Resilience and Persistence	203

INTRODUCTION

What is Business Growth?

It is more than increased sales, since extra sales may not increase profits. It is more than increased profits, because these might not be sustainable - customers might jump ship at the first opportunity – or you might not be generating positive cash flow.

Businesses need a healthy balance of sustainable profit and cash flow that will continue into the future.

If your business is based on one product that can become obsolete, then an important lever for growth is developing new products.

Growth definitely means building and keeping a winning team who will run the business successfully in your absence (occasional/permanent).

There are hundreds of reasons why businesses don't grow, and in most cases a variety of factors are present that stop a business reaching its' true potential, in the start-up phase as well as later stages. To identify and separate this mixture some in depth analysis may be required, for which an expert or at least a fresh pair of eyes may be needed.

It can also be a lack of systems and information that tells you on a timely basis how the business is doing. This area will always be a trade-off of costs and benefits. However no ship can sail without a compass and instruments to provide its bearings or it will never get to the destination and will risk perishing.

The challenges have been grouped into topics (departmental and transversal) without any special order or criteria except keeping a certain flow of thought thus making the points easier to understand.

As you read the 100 challenges you will find some overlaps, repetitions or you may consider some important points are missing. That is fine! There is no right or wrong here. Share you experience in our site (**www.BusinessGrowthLevers.com**) and contribute to the debate in the community.

This is our view based on 30 years of experience across 3 Continents.

From industry to industry and country to country there are particular complexities that make a substantial impact on the way a business functions. This is especially the case in employee situations where different practices in hiring, salaries and benefits and job protection legislation can have a significant impact.

This book is not intended to be an MBA in business, but a thought provocative guide to help businesses grow. Besides with the ever increasing rate of change nothing is static in business. Sometimes by the time a project is concluded changes in conditions have made it unviable. This is particularly true of High Tec (IT and Biotech) where many of the players of the 70s and 80s are no longer in existence, have ceased to be dominant or have changed significantly.

With globalization and information at their fingertips people have more choice as to products and suppliers. Businesses must learn to live with uncertainty, to anticipate cost fluctuations, trends and customer changes in demand and to continually improve and innovate their products and services if they want to thrive and not just survive.

Copying others or trying to adopt the latest management craze is unlikely to give better results than your competition is already getting. Flexibility, creativity and 'Thinking Outside the Box' solutions are essentials in this changing world.

Let us take you on a journey, a special journey in a time machine where you will be able to go back to the past and connect with it. This experience will help you gain awareness of the present and understand it better. You will also take a sneak peak of what the future may look like and gain clarity on the steps you need to start taking now to achieve the goals you set for your business and yourself.

Vision and Mission

All entrepreneurs start their companies because they have a **Vision** – their big idea, the dream of what their perfect business could be. They start full of optimism and energy yet, as Michael Gerber says, many of them are technicians or managers with an 'entrepreneurial seizure'.

This means their 'big idea' is to become their own boss doing basically the same thing they were doing in the previous company for whom they worked. Most of those are in the ranks of the 50% that do not survive the first 5 years, since they are not trained to run a company and they are usually adverse to delegation or seeking the help of experts in the various management competencies where they need support.

Others are better prepared or have done it before, and when they see the opportunity to serve a group of customers by providing a certain product or service and they think they will be able to do it better than anyone has done before, they go for it.

The **Vision Statement** defines the organization's long term purpose in terms of the values rather than the bottom line. It is a statement of what the organization wants to become, it provides shape and direction for the future. It needs to be short and to the point, not paragraphs or pages of waffle.

Values are usually the guiding beliefs about how things should be done within the organization. They are the core of what the organization is and cherishes. They give employees a framework as to how they are expected to behave and should inspire them to give their best. They will eventually shape the organization's culture.

When shared with customers and suppliers, values will act as the magnet that attracts or repels them and will shape their understanding of why they should buy or work with you.

A **Mission Statement** is a declaration of the core business and focuses on the main objectives. It expresses how the vision for the company is going to be fulfilled. Its prime function is as an internal document to define the key measure, or measures, of the organization's success.

Mission statements can (and should) also be written for departments or business units in alignment with the company's mission and vision so that the staff can participate and feel fully committed to what is stated.

A **Business Plan** is quite different, usually made in the start-up phase, or when a major expansion is planned, to get funding or partners.

The Vision and Mission Statements may be included in the Business Plan to give stakeholders a better understanding of the driving forces.

In www.success-academy.org/vision you will find Success Academy's Vision, Mission Statement and Values. I hope they will inspire you to write or review yours!

01 Getting a clear Vision

The entrepreneurs who started their business by jumping right in and doing what they were doing before, but 'as their own bosses' probably did not 'waste time' carefully designing their business. They may have totally overlooked writing down their Vision and Mission Statements even if they knew what they were. After all, they had work to do, products to build, clients to serve, so why 'waste time'?

Many business owners start up working alone, so if they didn't give much thought to verbalizing their Vision and Mission or get to writing them down, these concepts may have been too general or vague.

In that crucial first year they were not passed on to customers, suppliers and new employees as they joined.

Your vision statement should be clear, concise and inspiring enough to energize and motivate people inside and outside your organization. Why else would most large or medium sized companies have a Vision statement if they didn't add value?

The mission statement should state the measurable approach that makes your organization stand out from the crowd, which will be the reason why customers will come to you instead of your competitors.

As the company grows, having both a Vision and a Mission Statement becomes crucial.

Entrepreneurs may write them because someone advises them to, but unless they really buy into the importance of doing it, they will come up with generalities and platitudes that will not inspire anyone that has a relationship with the company. As the owner, you have to be an integral part of writing them so you really own the idea and the words.

It is never too late to create or revise a Vision Statement. Get your team involved so it is consensual, stimulates the organization's capabilities and confidence in the values it stands for. Combine the winning ideas with tangible, measurable goals and word it in a clear, concise statement and you will have your Mission Statement.

02 Establishing a Set of Values

Often we look around us and have the unpleasant feeling that ethics have gone out of fashion by the way we see people and organizations behave. Strangely enough this is not a symptom of lack of values, but the adoption of the wrong ones by taking shortcuts to increase profits and pursuing short term goals instead of building a sustainable business. Publicly quoted corporations have to publish quarterly reports because of Stock Exchange listings and in a rapidly changing world there is a lot of pressure to make a quick buck instead of build a sustainable income stream.

A solid set of values is an important part of the relationship between the company, its staff, its suppliers and its customers. If people respect what you stand for they are more likely to want to do business with you and work for you regardless of revenue and profit fluctuations.

Values represent for each individual personal their highest beliefs in life, so when the company they work for stands for the same sort of principles and has a well communicated code of ethics and conduct it is a powerful, winning combination.

Unfortunately businesses don't have a conscience and it is easier to slip into behaviors that are not noble and would not be condoned in an individual. Staff may not consider the long term benefit to the business and hence ignore the ethically correct course of action. The quick win and meeting the revenue or expense goals for the month or quarter usually takes precedence.

The banking sector in particular has been hurt by setting performance goals that incentivize staff to 'push' products onto clients. They are now seen as salesmen rather than professionals that can be relied upon for an objective opinion.

Values have to be lived up to on a day-to-day basis and be transparent throughout the organization. "One bad apple spoils the barrel" - if a customer is overcharged, the situation has to be promptly acknowledged and corrected, if an employee isn't paid for overtime he must be compensated in some other way that has perceived value, if a supplier is paid late a valid explanation must be given…

Negative feelings can turn a short-term gain into a long-term loss. Go above and beyond to maintain healthy, transparent relationships with employees, clients and suppliers.

Walk the talk, always over deliver on your promises and your company will grow on solid ground.

03 Common Goal

Failure to communicate the Vision, Mission or Values, or involve all of the staff as they are reassessed, will result in the lack of a common goal.

Unfortunately in many organizations if you asked different people what the company stands for or what is its most important value you would be surprised at the answers you would get.

A company, for many employees, is something abstract that they might see at best as "the boss's" business. Few know what the objectives are since they are either not made public or set out in such a way that the average person can't relate to them.

Does your company have a story, that every employee knows and that helps them identify with the business?

Is there something special about the history of the company, some unusual achievement?

Stories can be a very powerful way of communication that can humanize a company, making it more familiar - something they can have 'feelings' for and relate to and be proud of.

If you write your vision down on paper and share it with everyone you are increasing the chances of it becoming a reality.

This is firstly due to you taking it more seriously yourself – it is written down and shared (the accountability factor) – and secondly because if your staff buys into it they will be more motivated and inspired by what lies ahead, creating a sense of community and belonging which will impact performance and customer satisfaction.

How you communicate the goals and how often are also important. Putting it in the annual report or in the company newsletter that can be picked up at the factory door isn't enough. It should be displayed in plain sight on notice boards, included in every newsletter personally handed to employees and referred to in all speeches.

The same words should be in the company's website and in press releases where it will inspire potential new hires, new and existent customers and suppliers.

It needs also to be an integral part of the personalized welcome package that each member of staff gets when they join and get the induction training.

Your identity and what you stand for are part of your brand - it needs to be memorable and remembered.

04 Conviction

A Vision Statement sets out the challenge for the business and staff. It has to ring true to inspire and motivate everyone.

If your Vision Statement has been made a while ago do you still identify with what it says, or are you just going through the motions?

What is it that you doubt?

Do you doubt that these are still the right objectives for the future, do you doubt that they can be achieved, or do you doubt that the staff can be motivated by the vision? If you don't fully believe in the Vision Statement yourself, there are fundamental issues that have to be addressed first:

What is it about the Vision that feels wrong to you?

Do you have a conflict between your own values and where the business will go? For example you may have to turn a family business into something far less personal in order to expand.

Examining your feelings is not easy, but could be vital to getting yourself fully focused on the vision and mission.

Doubts about being able to achieve the objectives have to be broken down by keeping on asking yourself 'why do I think that' until you get to the bottom of it and you may find that there are, in fact, underlying problems.

If you feel something is not right, chances are that there is a reason you are not fully aware of at that moment. Trusting your gut may be hard to understand and accept but, as Malcolm Gladwell wrote in 'Blink', an "intuitive repulsion" for something that isn't right can be based on knowledge that can't be easily explained.

If you have trouble believing that you can motivate the staff what is causing this belief?

Is there a communication problem?

Do you need training or coaching?

Do you have the right people working for you?

Should the staff have some specific training so that they will understand the message better?

Does the Vision Statement need to be adapted or revised? If so, involve your team and get to work! You can't get a team motivated or performing at their best level around a vision that is no longer possible or inspiring!

Never get outsiders to write your Vision or Mission Statements for you! You may need help with getting clarity on the concept, but it needs to be your and your staff's words and ideas so that you really own them.

Clarity is crucial in any stage or decision of your life.

05 Too Grandiose or Not Ambitious Enough

While the Vision and Mission Statements are ideal means to set down in writing and communicate your dream for the future of the business, just a word of caution about getting carried away.

You are not verbalizing a utopian dream such as eradicating illness from the world! It is important that you stay in touch with what you can effectively achieve… If the vision sounds impractical or impossible, then it may not gain credibility and the status quo is likely to continue.

The main objective of the Vision is to inspire and motivate the staff. Hence employees should feel like they are part of something bigger than themselves, not that they are in 'Mission Impossible' because they won't feel committed and enthused.

You have to know in your heart, not just believe, that your Vision is possible to achieve some time in the future so that you can then convince your team.

At the other end of the spectrum if the Vision and Mission statements are lame or not ambitious enough it is almost as bad as not having them. Set mediocre goals and there will be under achievement, mediocre results. It will send the message to staff that there is no need to go the extra mile.

The goals need to be a challenge, outside (but of not too far outside) of the business comfort zone. Goals don't have to be about money.

Besides tactical goals, such as 'increase revenue by 50% over the next year' you can define strategic and more emotional objectives.

The term Big Hairy Audacious Goals (BHAG for short) is attributed to James Collins and Jerry Porras in their 1996 article 'Building Your Company's Vision'. An example of a BHAG is Microsoft's goal of 'A computer on every desk and in every home'.

This is an opportunity to inspire and you should use it so that your customers, suppliers and employees feel proud to be involved.

Being part of this vision should motivate your staff to give their best and stay with the project. When hiring, it should be a magnet to attract the top talents in the job market (not everyone goes for the job that offers the highest salary package).

Companies whose employees understand the mission and goals enjoy a 29% greater return than other firms (Watson Wyatt Work Study).

06 Lack of Strategy

Strategy is the 'HOW', a medium/long term approach that the organization takes to accomplish its Mission and move towards the Vision. The Strategy will be broken down into milestones, short term or annual goals and the Business Plan, with the necessary steps to accomplish the Mission.

Every business owner needs to understand the difference between Strategies and Tactics. Strategy is about the objectives and purpose. Tactics are about processes and actions.

You must determine your strategies for growth, consolidation, expansion, quality, etc., and only afterwards think through the tactics of how you are going to get there. If you rush into action or even set procedures without a Strategy behind you risk getting on the hamster wheel or running in circles without getting anywhere.

Tactics need to be the logical steps to achieve the goals. If you are not clear about the goal or what is the best overall plan to achieve it, you start taking aimless actions, sometimes recommended by well-meaning friends or advisors, and you end up doing the wrong things or what could be the right things but in the wrong order.

What do you do?

For whom do you do it?

How do you excel at it?

Never mistake motion for action, everything has to be thoroughly thought through. Priorities need to be set and conflicts resolved. If you try to maximize profit, you may restrict growth. You need to do the right things in the right order to be both effective and efficient.

As an entrepreneur or small business owner it all started with you or a small group of visionaries. Your company may have grown but some days you feel even worse than when you had a job because you can't quit, or things may still be going well but you don't feel the same enthusiasm and you know deep down that it shouldn't be this hard!

If you take the time to really think about your business and your life you will come to the conclusion that this is not just about the economic downturn (or even if it was, you couldn't do much about it). It comes down to YOU, to what you are going to do, because for things to happen and change YOU must change.

Vision and Mission

Main Takeaways:

1.

2.

3.

Improvements to implement:

Action 1.

By: Start Date: Ready by:

Action 2

By: Start Date: Ready by:

Action 3.

By: Start Date: Ready by:

You

You cannot change the tides or the direction of the wind. If a storm is coming, you may be able to decide to stay on shore if you haven't set sail yet, but once you've started the journey all you can do is adjust your course, set the sails and give it all you've got!

You may be overwhelmed by the complexity and the stress of the recession...

You may be struggling to get new clients or the business has just slowed down...

You may be so busy trying to make ends meet that you are neglecting your team...

Cash-flow may be a challenge... or you might be having trouble attracting the capital you need to grow...

You can only control your thoughts, the scenarios you build and the actions you take to achieve them.

Don't blame the weather or someone else for the results. If it doesn't work, try a new way since you can't get different results if you keep on applying the same solutions. The markets have changed; people's buying decisions have changed; so the only real question is 'What are YOU going to do about it?'

Take full responsibility for the results and keep taking the necessary steps to achieve the goals you set yourself to achieve. After all, when you started your aim was not only to create a great company but to create a great life for you and those around you!

In **www.BusinessGrowthLevers.com/resources** you will find a Self-Assessment Tool which can help you to gain clarity on where you are right now.

07 Knowing Where You Are

> *"Would you tell me, please, which way I ought to go from here?"*
> *"That depends a good deal on where you want to get to."*
> *"I don't much care where –"*
> *"Then it doesn't matter which way you go."*
> *Lewis Carroll, Alice in Wonderland*

This may seem like a stupid question to you and it may seem strange to place it here but since it is the starting point for improvement it has to be addressed right now!

Suppose you wanted to go to New York. That was the place where all your dreams would come true! You were given directions to get there from Miami... However, what if you were not in Miami? What if you were in Chicago? Would the directions be of any use to you?

How about being lost (pre-GPS)? You have a map but you don't know where you actually are, so you can't decide which road will take you where you want to go.

A compass is not going to be helpful unless you can see some landmarks and find them on the map. If you can find someone who speaks your language you may be able to discover which way to go, but can you trust their advice?

Where do you stand as a business owner? Do you feel lost, frustrated, overwhelmed, stuck or just uncertain of what to do next?

Do you know what are the specific things you need to change and the things that are holding you back? Do you have the skills, talent, knowledge and determination to make those changes?

What about the company? Do you know why customers have stopped buying or are buying less from you? What are they going to buy more of and from whom?

Do you have key performance indicators for each area of your business that show you where the money is coming from and where it is going?

What is the situation with your most valuable asset – your staff? Are they motivated or just doing the bare minimum because they can't afford to lose their jobs?

Stress caused by fear of losing your job is a major factor in health problems. Do they have personal issues (debt, spouses that have been made redundant, family illness that isn't covered by health insurance etc.) that are stopping them being energized and fully engaged?

Once you become clear on where you are you can get clearer on what your options are to get where you want to be and from there work towards the results you want to achieve.

08 Mindset

The first obstacles you may encounter along the way in your entrepreneurial journey are the ones that come from inside of you.

From the idea phase through the start-up period all the way to the maturity phase, the stories you tell yourself are going to play a major role in your success. Your mindset is an area that you need to learn to master by commitment and practice.

> *'This mind of mine went formerly wandering about as it liked, as it listed,*
> *as it pleased; but I shall now hold it in thoroughly,*
> *as the rider who holds the hook holds in the furious elephant.'*
> Buddha, Dhammapada, Chapter XXIII-326

What you think about has a direct impact in your level of success. If you focus on the problems you may feel helpless. If you focus on the solutions you will most likely find them.

Any skills or knowledge you may need along the way you can learn or obtain as long as you keep the right mindset. The same goes for your staff. Brains and talent are just the starting point and people can develop skills and self-discipline through repetition and hard work thus creating resilience that is essential for great accomplishment.

> *'You have to put your heart in the business and the business in your heart'*
> Thomas J. Watson Sr. (president of IBM 1952 – 1971)

Is your heart really in your business?

Do you really want to grow it or are you afraid of taking risks?

Do you feel passion for the industry, the company and the products?

Are you applying your greatest strengths and talents?

When it comes to personal empowerment, feeling mentally strong and grounded is crucial.

Think about your past wins and get in touch with a perception of yourself that sees you as strong and resilient. This will empower you in the face of adversities and setbacks.

Work on strengthening your mind by changing unproductive habits and focusing on being positive, having fun and being productive. Be resilient, but flexible. Be able to adapt to change and develop ways to handle the new paradigms. Look at all problems as challenges, puzzles to solve, obstacles to overcome, a chance to learn, exercise your mind and be creative.

While working on your mental strength do not neglect your physical and spiritual strengths. If you feel strong physically you will be more capable of coping with setbacks and your brain will be able to do its best work. Being spiritually strong will increase your level of awareness of yourself and others and you will feel more connected and balanced.

Set goals to capitalize on the opportunities you identify and work on minimizing the threats you find in your way. Don't complain about the obstacles that you encounter; keep on focusing on the results you want to achieve so that you overcome them.

09 Overcoming Fear

Taking your organization to the next level may require a radical change in how you do business and how you manage it. What is stopping you from taking that step?

Sit down with a pencil and paper and actually write down why you want to grow your business. Once you feel you have covered all the reasons write down the things that you think are stopping you.

There may be some underlying incongruences that are stopping you from really putting in your best effort.

Does the image of you in charge of a bigger and better company feel right or are you worried that you may not be able to cope? Is it fear of failure or fear of success?

Are you worried that if you set a goal and are not successful, others will criticize you or respect you less?

It is human to make mistakes. You should expect to fail and fall short many times before you achieve your goals. It is the normal process, the price to pay to achieve success. The harder the goal, the higher the price will be...

As Henry Ford once said:
"Failure is merely an opportunity to more intelligently begin again."

So failing is not the problem, it is how you react when you fail that will discourage or inspire the others. Make errors fast, learn the lesson and go for it again. You will achieve the objectives you set a lot faster.

The best way to develop courage and confidence is with knowledge and skill. When you learnt how to drive it was overwhelming - the number of things you had to watch out for and all the things you had to do with your hands and feet! After a few months of regular practice you were so competent at driving that you could do it well without even thinking about it.

It is also important to have control over your emotional state by choosing not to allow external influences upset you. Don't look for validation from others, look for cooperation; get into the habit of stepping back emotionally and challenging beliefs that don't serve you.

How do you feel about earning a lot more money, or even being rich? Although money is a byproduct of your success, you should be clear about any negative feelings you may have around it.

Money is not evil or selfish. Money is neutral. It is what you do with it that determines who you are. You can use it to grow your business, to help others and to make the world a better place to live in.

If you have lost your passion and do not care about your business, your staff or your customers soon it will reflect negatively in the business (even if you think you put on a good act).

Enthusiasm is contagious but so is lack of enthusiasm. You should consider pulling out if the company can survive without you, getting someone else to lead the business or finding a way to reconnect with your initial passion.

10 Being a better Leader

Leadership is a vast subject. Many books have been written about it and many will follow as new research and trends emerge.

There are different styles of leadership which can be more or less effective depending upon the situation - if the ship is sinking you don't ask for votes.

Leadership has evolved from being based on task specific expertise to depending upon personal, interpersonal and strategic skills.

In any shape or form leadership starts within you, in the clarity you have on your goals and in the understanding you have of yourself and others. It is an ongoing growth process, but it is a learnable one.

Be honest with yourself and have the humility to search for the help of others or invest in developing leadership skills. This will pay big time because leadership creates results and that is what you want for your business.

The best leaders are those who can tap into the emotions of others and get them to reach a level they wouldn't have reached on their own. For that they must show they value the work and opinion of each member of the team and give them room to be creative and responsible.

If the members of your team feel inspired and appreciated by you, they will feel totally engaged and perform at their best.

With time and practice you will master the art of identifying other people's hot buttons and your own. Knowing yours is vital, because on the positive side it will help you to stay motivated and on the downside it will help you to avoid engaging in behaviors that you will regret later.

Following are some examples of poor leadership:

Being indecisive - rushing decisions can be dangerous if you have not weighed all the facts and heard the opinions of the people involved or affected; however many time the leader has to make a quick assessment of the risks and take the responsibility for the choice made (the best with the information available). Building consensus is important for long term motivation but a balance has to be found between the level of urgency and the risk and importance.

Not setting clear expectations – everybody in the organization needs to be clear on what is expected of them, by when, and where to get help. All results must be measurable so that people's performance can be evaluated fairly.

Killing the messenger – people must not be afraid of reporting a potential problem or admitting responsibility for an error. The penalty for not communicating has to be greater than the consequences they will have to face if they own up, or management may only become aware of situations once they have become difficult or impossible to solve.

Taking all of the glory – replacing the 'me' by 'us' goes a long way to motivating your followers. Everyone should be encouraged to contribute with constructive ideas or people won't feel engaged and mediocrity can soon become the normal state of affairs.

Not taking responsibility – as a leader you can't forget that YOU are ultimately responsible for all that happens or doesn't happen in the business. If you allow people to be recruited without the appropriate skills, don't ensure they get the right training, information and resources, you will be letting everyone down. Even if you feel you couldn't have done any better, accepting responsibility will set the example for others to feel accountable for their actions.

11 Being a better Listener

'Most conversations are simply monologues delivered in the presence of witnesses'
Margaret Miller

You are the boss, you speak and people listen. Right?

There are very few instances where you do not have to receive information from other people to be able to run a business. Unfortunately there is often a tendency to cut in with questions or refute information before the speaker has finished. This can cause nervousness or loss of train of thought and some vital data might not be delivered or its context and relevance clearly explained.

There are many reasons why people fail to listen properly. They may be distracted by an activity they are attempting to do whilst listening, have other thoughts in their heads they deem to be more important, or they may be thinking about what they are going to say next.

The listener's opinion of the speaker, as a person, may also influence the extent to which they are happy to pay attention and give their time. This may be based on simple likes and dislike or on status.

Don't prejudge the speaker. Even if the first words rankle with you wait until they finish before making any decisions. Some people do not express themselves too well and only by listening to all that is said will you get a full understanding of the point they were trying to make.

Don't feel uncomfortable with silence. Be patient and wait. Do not assume or allow preconceptions to wreck communications.

While a written report may give you valuable detail that you may not be able to assimilate while listening, a verbal report could help with a more intuitive insight.

Besides the actual words you need to pay attention to the tone of voice and body language.

If you are in a meeting and a Sales Manager is telling you his projections for the next month you may feel when he is not fully committed to achieving those results. This could be because of the words used, the lack of enthusiasm in his voice, the way he avoids looking you in the eyes or the general body language.

Listening will help you to understand other people's needs and wants. Then you can tailor your message to them.

This also applies to clients. How can you sell them anything if you don't listen to their needs?

... to suppliers – how can you negotiate with them if you can't create a win-win situation?

... to your partners or shareholders – how can you see their perspective if you don't listen to them?

... and above all to your staff – how can you lead a team if you don't know them?

A business depends on human interaction to succeed.

Interaction starts with the quality of your listening, so make sure that interaction will be of the highest caliber.

12 Being a better Speaker

*'A talk is a voyage. It must be charted.
The speaker who starts nowhere, usually gets there.'*
Dale Carnegie

Although listening is considered by many more important than speaking, if you can't communicate your thoughts in a clear and objective way you can confuse your listener.

To get your company and its products known it is usually best to get all of the good media exposure that you can get.

If you have trouble speaking in public you can always use a spokesperson or issue a press release, although coming straight from you and straight from the heart is the best way to go.

Do you have trouble at times thinking on your feet or making speeches? Speaking, especially in public, is one of the most common fears.

Some people resort to techniques such as NLP or individual coaching. For most people, however, practicing in the right environment will help them overcome this challenge. Toastmasters International (www.toastmasters.org) is a worldwide non-profit club for learning to speak in public where a structured program is followed to learn various aspects of being a good communicator.

Whether you are speaking internally or externally, to one person or a large audience, there are some basic rules it is wise for you to follow.

Decide exactly what you want to accomplish before you start talking.

Make it easy for the listeners to follow your ideas - use words that they can understand and their jargon if you are talking to a specific profession group.

If possible use images, stories or jokes to maintain engagement, increase retention and make the message more compelling. Speak with enthusiasm and connect emotionally - don't be afraid to be human.

Be aware of your body language and of what it is communicating to your audience.

Pay attention to their body language. Are they engaged?

Be sure to explain 'what is in it for them' - the benefits of taking this action, buying this product, following this instruction.

Keep it reasonably short so that you don't bore them or make them feel it is a waste of everybody's time.

Find a way to have them participate by raising their arms in answer to a question or standing up. Make sure you allow space for questions or clarification requests at the end (or before breaks if there are any).

If you are addressing a group, giving a presentation or a speech, make sure you have an attention grabbing opening, you make clear points, summarize them at the end and close with a call to action or explanation of what the next steps are going to be.

If you use technology like a power point presentation, make it a support, not a distraction.

Practice, practice, practice!

Communication is the key to every relationship and speaking is not so much about what you say but about the message that the others perceive you are passing on to them.

Think about this and always prepare before you address an audience no matter how small it may be.

13 Being a better Negotiator

Do you feel at ease when you are negotiating? What is usually the outcome?

Do you ever feel that a partner, supplier, client or employees have taken advantage of you?

Do you struggle to get what you want?

A good negotiator gets the right deal, what is really needed for the correct price. A bad negotiator doesn't get what is needed, pays too much for it or both.

Another way of being a bad negotiator is to drive too hard a bargain and exploit the other person so that they can't fulfill the agreement or won't want to do business again in the future. Even if it is just a one-time deal the word might get around and make negotiations with others more difficult. You have to think about the future, not just this deal.

A negotiation in the broad sense can be a dialogue between two or more people or parties with the intention to resolve a point of difference or reach an agreement upon a course of action.

Negotiation skills are as useful at work as they are in your private life or even at home (any parent will attest to that!). A skilled negotiator not only knows how to use techniques, but also how to recognize them in the other party.

It is always important to prepare for a negotiation. The extent of the preparation should be proportional to the importance of the issue or the financial impact it may have. Be clear on your goals and write them down in order of priority. Research the other party's background and motivations so that you evaluate as clearly as possible their goals.

What do each of you have that the other wants?

What is the issue on the table?

Are there alternative scenarios?

What are the consequences for each?

What is the past history?

Which party has more leverage/power?

What compromises could be reached?

Be clear on what concessions you are willing to make and what will be your 'walk away' point (the most you are prepared to give to get what you need). Be comfortable with the idea that it may come to this point.

During the negotiation do not make assumptions, never take anything personally, and move towards the objective slowly making concessions one at a time. Remember that for a negotiation to be 'win-win', both parties should feel positive about the negotiation once it's over.

If you ignore your 'walk away' point there can be a risk that you will settle for a loose-win deal because you want it to happen too much. Even if you have invested a lot of time and money (e.g. travel, hotels, consultants etc.) and have become emotionally attached to what things will look like after the deal, be prepared to walk away.

Until you feel you can master your emotions and the negotiation techniques you should never go into an important negotiation alone.

> *'The best executive is the one who has sense enough to pick good men to do what he wants done, and self-restraint enough to keep from meddling with them while they do it.'*
> Theodore Roosevelt

14 Being a better Problem Solver

A problem is nothing but a challenge, a chance to make things better. Hence problem solving is a key skill for avoiding bad decision making.

Once you have developed an efficient process of approaching the issues, you will be capable of solving problems quickly and effectively and you will be confident facing any road blocks that come your way.

Do you examine the various aspects of problems, various solutions and their implications and possible effects?

Do you make sure you are addressing the real problem and not the symptoms?

The way we deal with problems usually reflects our nature, unless we make a conscious effort to behave differently. Some of us rush in, find the first likely solution, make a quick decision and move on; others analyze everything in minute, fully documented detail; finally there are the ones who ignore the problem altogether.

The essential step you need to take before anything else is to identify and define the problem and make an assessment of its magnitude. Is it a significant or potentially significant problem that you yourself have to deal with, can you delegate all or part of it, or can it be ignored?

Next step is to analyze the problem in appropriate detail, separating the symptoms from the causes so that solutions can be generated.

Obviously, the more complex the problem is, the more difficult it can be to identify realistic solutions and you may have to get expert help. In any case, getting to the root causes is essential for finding the best solution.

For example, a problem such as a lack of sales could be due to lack of sales leads, inability to close sales, or both. Within each of these, many possibilities can exist individually or combined - inability to close sales could be due to the product (price, quality or availability) or to the salesmen (motivation, training or availability). Analysis of the problem could include gathering data, such as quantifying the conversion rate of sales leads and then quantifying different reasons for failure to convert.

Once you have broken down the problem into all the different variables, you need to identify steps that can be taken immediately to start solving it.

Looking for solutions needs to be viewed by everyone in the company as a creative challenge. You can use several techniques to come up with alternative solutions. Two that are widely used are brainstorming and lateral thinking.

Brainstorming is a group creativity technique where the group tries to find a solution for a specific problem by gathering spontaneously generated ideas.

Lateral thinking is an indirect creative approach using reasoning that is not immediately obvious. It involves ideas that may not be obtained by using only traditional step-by-step logic. These ideas for solutions then need to be evaluated as to their advantages and constraints so that they can be prioritized. There may not be adequate resources (money or manpower) for some or the implementation time may be too long.

Always involve the members of your staff who are key to the issue at hand since if they don't 'buy in' to the changes they may resist and even sabotage the implementation.

Once you have decided on the course of action, be clear as to WHO has to do WHAT and by WHEN.

15 Being a better Manager

Leaders lead and managers manage, but a good leader needs some management skills (or all of them if he is also the manager) and a manager needs some leadership skills to be able to work with the team.

Leadership is about WHAT and WHY. Management is about HOW.

Leadership is about innovation, people and trust. Management is about systems, controls, procedures, policies and structure.

The manager relies on control, has more of a short-term view and has his or her eyes always on the bottom line.

Poor leaders are despots, while poor managers are bureaucrats in the worst sense of the word.

Leading is about effectiveness. Managing is about efficiency.

As your business starts to grow and you have to hire staff, brush up your management skills and make sure you don't fall into these very common errors:

Expecting too much of staff - just because people work for you it doesn't make them psychic or able to do anything without proper training. Each person has different levels of talent, skills, experience.

A task that could be given to one person with complete confidence might be a disaster if given to someone else. Imagine asking a trainee to analyze the clients' receivables ageing. He may not know what that is, much less how to analyze it. I knew a CEO who could not do a simple math addition. You have to know your staff and their capabilities.

Failing to provide clear directions - don't assume that staff know what to do. Be clear about your expectations, establish clear priorities and make sure they understand how their performance is going to be measured. Explain, educate and inform.

Overloading staff with more work than they can handle - if you are a workaholic, be aware that other people have a life outside your company. Overtime may be required occasionally, but over long periods it will compromise efficiency and staff motivation, not to mention creating stress and health issues.

Insufficient challenge for employees - learning or doing something new brings motivation and fulfillment for most people, provided they are not taken too far out of their comfort zone. Absence of new challenges can cause boredom and productivity decline.

Lack of attention to detail - often a single seemingly insignificant factor can bring about a huge change in the outcome of an event. Focus on what is critical for success.

Micro managing - giving a task to someone and then checking up on them far more than needed. Interruptions will result in them taking more time on the task, can demotivate them and may restrict their creativity because they feel you don't trust them. They will 'play safe' by doing what is expected instead of developing their own ideas of how it can be done more efficiently.

Being afraid to show you are human - acknowledging your own mistakes when you make them will make is easier for the staff to speak up and make suggestions without fear of the consequences. If you act like you are always right and they are afraid of you, they'll stay quiet and conceal theirs faults too.

Lack of feedback - if you don't follow up and let your staff know how they have performed, they will most likely continue to perform poorly. On the other hand, lack of feedback for good performance causes the performance to drop because the person either doesn't know if they are performing well or they feel unappreciated.

Listen to your staff, show you appreciate them and make them feel like people instead of just a piece of the machine that makes you money. Keep it professional though, so that you are seen as objective and fair and can deal promptly with uncomfortable issues either by coaching or mentoring the staff that need it or, in extreme cases, by ending the relationship with minimum impact in the performance of the company.

16 Coping better with Stress

The effect of sudden stress is usually acceleration of your pulse rate as you get into a 'fight or flight mode' with accompanying releases of hormones and adrenaline. The analytical part of the brain actually shuts down as you move into a state where you have no time to ponder the situation but have to react. Muscles receive a burst of energy and you either fight the saber-tooth tiger or try to out-run it. This is the 'instinctive reaction' that can save your life by making you jump when you are crossing the road and see a car coming towards you.

In your day-to-day job your stress level may increase due to different circumstances - difficulties with customers, production, staff or financial problems. Your personal life can also suffer because you may still be stressed when you get home. Your ability to get a good nights' sleep may be compromised, which leaves you tired and in a worse state to deal with the stress of the following day. It becomes a vicious circle where it gets harder to cope and you'll make more mistakes, get angry and probably say things that you later regret.

You may think it is 'normal'… after all this is the worse economic downturn in modern times… or you may be saying to yourself "it is just a rough patch" and compensate it with pills or by smoking or drinking more.

Stress management starts with accepting you are stressed and identifying the sources of stress in your life.

If your methods of coping with stress aren't contributing to your emotional and physical health, it's time to find healthier ones.

Avoid people who stress you out because they are negative or just because they get on your nerves. Know your limits and learn when to say 'No'.

Avoid situations or topics that may upset you from watching the news to discussing politics or even sports.

Manage your time better and be flexible. Compromise and avoid bottling up negative feelings.

Focus on the positive and look at the big picture. Don't waste your time with unnecessary details.

Adjust your standards if needed, as long as the change doesn't affect the end result or compromise your values.

Don't try to control the uncontrollable. Acceptance may be difficult, but in the long run, it's easier than flailing against a situation over which you have no influence.

Nurture yourself and make time for fun and relaxation. Learn some techniques like yoga, meditation, or just deep breathing routines. You will be in a better place to handle the challenges as they come.

Adopt a healthy lifestyle - exercise regularly, eat a healthy diet, avoid alcohol and pills and get enough sleep so that you can deal with problems head on and with a clear mind.

It is important that you find out what works best for you in each situation and that you don't let it get out of hand.

Being around like minded, positive people, exercising and having a few laughs is a great antidote for stress.

17 Dealing with Change

> *'Your success in life isn't based on your ability to simply change. It is based on your ability to change faster than your competition, customers and business.'*
> *Mark Sanborn*

Today, perhaps the most important factor affecting our lives is the speed of change.

We are living in an age where change is taking place at a faster rate than ever before and happening in irregular patterns and unpredictable directions. Change is coming from all sides and in so many different ways that it is often impossible to anticipate what may happen next.

Business owners are often faced with the problem of seeing their very best plans and ideas destroyed overnight as the result of a completely new and unexpected development. It is hard to cope with the situation but the extent of the consequences depends totally on your capability to analyse quickly, plan and implement, since you have to be in control of the steps you take and not be pushed around by the circumstances.

The best way is to involve all your staff in monitoring any changes in the market to identify trends that may impact the business. Your organization has to be flexible enough to respond quickly and set adequate actions in motion including the realignment of staff, resources and capacity.

Change causes enormous stress for people who are fixed or rigid in their beliefs about how things 'should be.' Actions that have worked in the past, systems that have done wonders for your company and were pivotal to your success may have to be totally scrapped.

Part of the fear of change comes from dealing with the unknown and this is why communication is especially important when you are going through change. A lack of dialog can have a negative impact, while effective communication can make the process easier.

You need details about the change, so that you can determine how it affects you. Don't just sit back and wait for things to happen.

Ask yourself continuously: "Will these actions or procedures continue to work efficiently under the new circumstances? Is it achieving the end results desired?" If the answer is 'No', be prepared to change.

Make changes not just for the sake of it or impulsively but after brainstorming, listening to your staff and maybe external experts so that your course of action achieves the result or goal you have set.

Survival depends on being constantly alert for new ideas, information or knowledge that can help or hurt your business or the accomplishment of your goals. You need to be quicker and smarter than your competitors and always be working on ways to make your product or service a better experience for your customer.

With the right positive attitude and actions plus the flexibility to reinvent yourself and your business you will find opportunities in the market changes instead of regarding them as frightening and disruptive.

18 What if You were Abducted by an Alien?

A lot of businesses fail not because the owner doesn't work enough but because he is working too hard doing the wrong type of work.

As an Entrepreneur you should ask yourself if the business would be able to survive without you and work on building a business that could.

The reasons are obvious. You probably started the business because you wanted more freedom (not to be a slave), you may want to sell it eventually and you want a source of income for your family even if you are temporarily absent (on holiday or for a less happy reason).

Do you believe that you are the only one who can do some of the key tasks correctly?

Do you feel you need to be in control of everything that is going on?

Does the need to be in control stop you from delegating?

Do you feel more successful if you have a lot to do and are always pushing yourself?

Remember that 'busy' is very different from 'efficient' and 'productive'.

Micromanagers often justify their approach with a simple experiment: they give a member of staff an assignment they usually take care of themselves and then disappear until the deadline. The person struggles with no clear instructions and lack of experience, so the result is far from brilliant which 'proves' the micromanager's point. What they can do in one hour takes everyone else two and it is done badly…

If you don't provide appropriate training to your staff, trust them, give clear instructions and adequate supervision to perform tasks, they will feel disempowered and you will have failed both as leader and manager.

Disempowered employees are ineffective and require a lot of time and energy from whoever is in charge to resolve problems and ensure work is being done. Focus first on the ones with the most potential and learn to delegate effectively to them.

Start by delegating small tasks and, when these have been mastered, increase their size and complexity. Encourage them to set goals as they progress with the task. This will increase their ownership of the process. Remember that listening to their input is important.

Give them clear information about your desired results. Offer clear and measurable objectives. Communicate fully the reason for the task and the consequences if the task is not carried out successfully.

Great delegation is about delegating an outcome rather than dumping a problem on someone else. It does not imply lack of control. With the right systems in place engaged employees produce amazing results and you can continue handling the critical tasks that require your brilliance.

You must take some time every week to be away from the day to day routine with the sole intention of looking at the business objectively. There are many things you can do during this time, from reconnecting with your vision to pondering strategies and designing new systems or redesigning old ones.

If you are not doing this systematically, the business is running you, instead of YOU running the business.

It is imperative that as the business grows you spend more of your time working 'on' the business, than 'in' the business. This gives you the opportunity to assess, evaluate and identify new improvements, possibilities and ideas. It's the difference between having a job or the success you truly want.

19 Poor Health

"To keep the body in good health is a duty...
otherwise we shall not be able to keep our mind strong and clear."
Buddha

So, what if you haven't been abducted by aliens, but you have the flu? Will the company survive without you for 2 or 3 days? Do you tough it out and hope not to pass it on to the rest of your staff, or do you go home to bed and leave them to cope? If you stay at work remember you won't be firing on all cylinders, so performance will be affected. It is difficult to think clearly when ill or under medication.

The company must be able to survive without you! That said, there are stages (startup or transitions), and occasions (important negotiations or meetings) where your absence may result in financial losses or compromise the future of the business.

This is why having you performing at your best is so important for the company - your health can affect the bottom line! You need to make the effort to stay fit since your health is part of the business's assets.

Being fit is much more than how good you look (although a fat and sloppy CEO or a pale and run-down one do not convey the right image for the business, whatever the product or service may be).

It is about being energized and performing at your best level, it is a combination of eating habits, exercise and rest.

Each person responds differently to certain foods or diets. Finding out what you have too little or too much of and getting into balance is a first step. No one is asking you to take drastic measures unless your health is at risk. Giving up or cutting back on foods that are not right for you can be a challenge and affect your mood negatively. Adjust your mindset and work slowly but firmly in the right direction, just like when you started your business. The results will pay off. Hydration is also paramount. An immune system that functions well is essential.

Physical activity, like the right diet, has to be personalized. It will be a challenge when you start, especially if you are out of shape. If you are not keen on going to the Gym there are exercises you can do at the office desk or at home. Since you have to do it on a regular basis, choose things that you enjoy doing, like walking, swimming, playing baseball with your kids and do them in places you like such as the beach, a park or the mountains.

Take the stairs instead of the elevator if it is only one or two floors and get up to get your own coffee, or preferably water. This last one will give you a chance to stretch, rest your eyes (if you work many hours on the computer) and see what the staff are doing (added bonus).

Another good option is to exercise in a group. This way you get the support of accountability partners which will improve your motivation and will be an opportunity for networking at the same time.

Rest is the final important piece of the health puzzle to relieve stress and repair the body. Regular sleep patterns are important for both your mind and your body. A dark room, without electronic devices that produce radio or electromagnetic radiation that disrupt brain waves is best for sleeping deeply. Clear your mind of anything which might stop you sleeping before turning the lights off. If there is something important you don't want to forget, make a note of it so that you will deal with it in the morning.

20 Loneliness

Being the boss can get very lonely, with the number of people that we can confide in (especially at a personal level) becoming less and less as the business grows. Additionally, having the ultimate responsibility for every aspect of the organization can be overwhelming.

Most decisions require the consideration of many different factors, some of which you may not feel qualified to evaluate. Talking about a situation would help you gain clarity since it has to be 'materialized' into words when explaining it to the other person. In most cases, the input you get from your staff is invaluable. They are your team and in the best position to know the challenges the company is facing.

What about your personal challenges? What about the doubts you may have sometimes as to whether you will be able to handle it or you really want to?

What about the pressure to respond quicker and smarter to market changes than your competitors?

Many business owners and executives find a mentor, coach or mastermind group to help them cope with these challenges.

A Mentor has the advantage of having been there and done it. Practical experience and a proven track record can give you confidence in their opinion. Less time will be needed to explain to him or her the intricacies of the industry or the business.

The difficult task can be finding a mentor who is up to date in terms of new developments. What got them there in the past may not work now or in the future, and what worked for them may not work for you because you have different values and objectives.

A Coach should work with you in a different way, asking questions so that you reflect on the issues, examine your values, challenge your assumptions hence gaining clarity. Working with a Coach may be one on one or in a group, either in person or over the phone. Unfortunately there are a lot of people calling themselves Coaches who have had little or no training. When choosing a Coach make sure the person is qualified and above all that you feel empathy and trust so there is a safe space for you to open up.

A Mentor-coach is someone who has been through the same sort of challenges but that will use coaching tools to help you. The advantages are that empathy is usually established quicker, especially if you share similar business values and the Coach's input in a brainstorming session is more qualified.

Mastermind groups have become widespread. A Mastermind group comprises a number of business people from different industries who discuss each other's challenges. Often they are moderated by a Coach and can be an excellent source of knowledge and support both in the form of resources and in providing accountability.

Whichever the right solution is for you, it can end the feeling of being alone and accelerate the process of attaining sustainable results in a significant way. You won't know how much it will do for you until you have tried it...

21 Do You Know Where You Want to Go?

Does this point seem redundant, especially since we have already examined 'Knowing Where You Are'?

We have talked about the Vision Statement and the Mission Statement. They reflect where your organization is going and the general path to get there. However, change happens every day.

When was the last time your Strategic Plan was reviewed? And the Business Plan? Do you do it systematically? Who is involved in the process? Are the results communicated throughout the organization?

Being in charge of a startup or early stage business is a very different job from running a mature organization. All businesses have a natural lifecycle and go through different periods of growth with very different challenges for the Entrepreneur to overcome. To understand the priorities and challenges at each stage is vital for the health and survival of the organization.

In the start-up stage you are normally working long hours in the business. There is excitement; your energy is usually high. You need to attract clients, build a reputation and establish a solid cash-flow.

In the growth stage everything gets more complicated – you have staff, production, customer issues, etc. that are day to day problems to solve. Many organizations struggle or decline in this stage. You must decide what your own role should be, reassess how your company is positioned in the market place and whether your vision is still realistic in the current economic conditions.

Does expansion into new markets still make sense? Is staying in the current segment still the best option? What new skills and tools should be acquired to make the process smoother?

Now is the time to build the capabilities your business will need in the future and this is getting to be a huge challenge as the future is proving to be more and more unpredictable.

An effective way to make sure your road maps are still valid is to keep a permanently updated SWOT analysis for your business (as the owner you may want to keep one for your personal life too). The SWOT analysis will give you more clarity over the adequacy of both your strategy – how you are planning to achieve your goals and your tactics - the actions you have designed to achieve them.

If external or internal circumstances change, you may decide the tactics have to change, or you may have to re-evaluate the strategy with your team. In either case clarity is paramount and you can only be clear about how to run your business if you are aware of what is going on around you, where your company stands and how it can be impacted by what is happening. This includes information on technology, best practices or legislation that will affect your industry, the market and your organization.

To run a successful, efficient, effective and profitable business you need Systems, KPIs (key performance indicators) and a great team.

So let's focus now on the business itself.

Main Takeaways:

1.

2.

3.

Improvements to implement:

Action 1.

By: Start Date: Ready by:

Action 2.

By: Start Date: Ready by:

Action 3.

By: Start Date: Ready by:

Business Plans

'If you fail to plan, you plan to fail' - this quote is attributed to several authors, which makes its message even stronger.

A Business Plan is a road map for your organization. It establishes the company's value proposition for customers, partners/investors and both present and future employees. It is also an indispensable tool for obtaining financing from the banking system.

A clear and realistic business plan gives your organization credibility and will develop the interest of potential investors or business partners. It can also be used when hiring senior staff to give them the confidence that the business is viable and has a defined path.

In **www.BusinessGrowthLevers.com/resources** you will find a Business Plan structure and other tools you can use in your business.

22 Not having a Plan

My uncle is a house builder in Australia and he admires the carpentry skills of the Aborigines who have a 'feeling' for wood. Their work is of excellent quality, however they have a major disadvantage as employees - they occasionally go 'walk-about'. They would disappear for a few days or a few months without warning and just go wherever their fancy takes them, living rough in the bush or with friends and relatives.

He could not be sure when a house would be ready; therefore he did not know when he was going to get paid. He had to plan the construction factoring in the risk of not having carpenters available at the right time. Hence he had his plan for building a house with the most efficient sequence and his contingency plan depending on when he could get carpenters.

A few years ago The Wall Street Journal published an article with the title: 'Do Startups Really Need Formal Business Plans?' It cites research that questions the need for Business Plans for all startups. It tells stories of would-be entrepreneurs who failed despite their seemingly impeccable Business Plans and stories of successful startups without any Business Plans. The thought behind the article was that markets, technology and other variables change so much quicker nowadays that if you spend too long planning, by the time you finish circumstances will have changed and your plan will be inadequate, if not totally obsolete. On the other hand, some intuitive or seasoned Entrepreneurs have followed their 'gut feeling' and succeeded.

Both over-planning and leaving it to 'instinct' are poor strategies. You need a guideline, although the plan in itself means very little and does not guarantee success.

Business Plans are tools stating a path to follow and must be updated as you go. They are living things based on assumptions that should be monitored and adjusted to reality.

The big advantage is that a Business Plan will keep you focused on the result and what it will look like when you get there.

Even for businesses that evolve in a completely unplanned way because of special circumstances, skills, knowledge or particular niche, there usually comes a time when reorganization is needed - larger premises, more staff, expansion to new markets or an overhaul of the original strategy. The Business Plan will give you a basis to start working, by comparing it to the current reality so you can build from there.

Everyone joining a new organization needs time to get to know the company, its values, systems, products, colleagues, etc. This process will be a lot easier if the fundamentals are laid out in a concise plan.

Success is made of many factors – opportunity, persistence, timing, luck, etc. With no map you will be drifting and need a lot more luck to leverage your strengths and pursue your passion the most efficient way.

An intuitive, creative and flexible Entrepreneur will be better equipped to succeed, but if he relies only on his ability to 'wing it' with all the challenges he is faced with, he is leaving a lot of potential on the table.

23 Unclear or Incomplete Planning

A survey showed that many small-business owners wished they had had more capital and financial management education at the outset.

The more the company grows, the bigger the need for written planning so that the team can understand the company's values, work for the common goals, understand the customers and competitors and focus on important issues like Profit and Growth.

If an Entrepreneur puts a Business Plan together just to get financing or because he thinks he is 'supposed to' without understanding why, the document may be unclear or incomplete and will not be the useful tool it is supposed to be for running the company.

A Business Plan should set the goals and objectives for the company's performance, provide a basis for evaluating and controlling that performance and to communicate the company's message to middle managers, directors, lenders, potential investors and other stakeholders.

The most common structure starts with an Executive Summary - concise explanation of the business, description of the market size and market need for the business and an explanation of how the company is uniquely qualified to fulfill this need.

Afterwards there will be a Business Description - industry, future possibilities and how the business is going to be profitable, the Market Strategies - positioning, market share, pricing, distribution and promotion plan, the Competitive Analysis, the Design and Development Plan - product development and risk assessment, the Operation and Management Plan - logistics and organizational structure and the Financial Projections.

If you did not prepare a Business Plan before you started operations (or just had a very basic one) and your company has grown healthy, congratulations, you were both efficient and lucky! Consider that an incentive for preparing a Business Plan for the next 3 to 5 years and include some data of your company's history (profile, past accomplishments and unique qualifications).

Preparation of Business Plans can be based on existing data using a bottom up approach or built with a top down approach. In a bottom up approach, if you wanted to increase sales by say 10%, theoretically you could achieve this with 10% more fully trained staff in place. However, you may find that you have sufficient staff who, with extra training could handle 10% more sales.

Is the increase in sales going to be via an increase in customers or by selling more to existing customers?

Will there be a price increase or a change in the product mix included in the plan?

Depending upon the nature of your business there may have to be a dialogue between Sales, Marketing, HR, Finance, Production (or Procurement) and Logistics, if these departments exist. This approach tends to refine the way business is done to achieve better results.

A top down approach is where you set the overall objectives, then each department has objectives and the heads of the departments have to come up with a plan and justify what they need to reach these results.

This can lead to a more aggressive allocation of resources especially if you have industry data to use as a benchmark. Consequently, there can be considerable changes in how business is done rather than a refining process of the existing systems as per the bottom up approach.

24 Over Planning

You may not have got into 'analysis paralysis' yet, but it is something worth avoiding. Vast amounts of time can be spent on preparing the perfect plan, examining all contingencies, integrating it for all aspects of the business with buy-in and reality checks. However, while you and your team are doing all this, you are taking time away from the day to day running of the business.

If you think putting the Business Plan together is taking up too much time and resources, consider asking for the help of professionals. Consultants are the only ones that make money out of Business Plans but they can save money for your business. Use them for putting your ideas onto paper. The Plan must come from you (and your staff) and should never be outsourced completely.

As said before, a Business Plan is a tool, not an end in itself. The idea is not to create the perfect Business Plan but create the Perfect Business!

Don't use a Business Plan to show how much you know about your business. Nobody reads a long-winded Business Plan - neither bankers nor venture capitalists! Years ago they may have been impressed by long plans, but too much information is time consuming and gets stale due to the speed at which markets, products and technology change.

As an internal document the Business Plan needs to be complete, but it will be hard to implement unless it is simple, specific and realistic. Minute or trivial items that dilute or mask the critical aspects of the plan should be avoided.

A plan also needs to be flexible. You need to be able to adapt it quickly to whatever changes come your way. The moment you try to make the perfect plan, you trap yourself into a habit of forever updating the plan instead of doing something about it. And that is simply procrastinating. So, stop it. And start doing!

Finally, never make the mistake of being a slave to what you have written in your Business Plan. Once all of the planning has been done there may be too many things to measure and check and the monthly report may become so detailed you don't have time to wade through it. Concentrating on a few key indicators and numbers is all that is needed to understand how the business is progressing against the Plan.

Take the Capital budget, for example. If you know you will be adding 10 office staff, then there will be a need for 10 desks, chairs, computers, phones, etc. Purchasing should give you the cost per person, possibly with IT separate if it is the IT manager who is responsible for that part of the budget. Any exceptions need to be clearly identified. Then if only 8 people are hired, it is quite linear that only 80% of the budget should have been spent, give or take any variations in the pricing.

25 Contingencies Not Studied

> *"I tell this story to illustrate the truth of the statement I heard long ago in the Army: Plans are worthless, but planning is everything. There is a very great distinction because when you are planning for an emergency you must start with this one thing: the very definition of 'emergency' is that it is unexpected, therefore it is not going to happen the way you are planning."*
> Dwight Eisenhower

When you are preparing a Plan, there are a lot of unknown factors that could have a major impact on its achievement. These could include external factors like inflation, currency fluctuations, economic slowdowns and legislation, or internal factors like a strike, hackers entering your computer systems, legal actions, fire and natural disasters or the loss of a major customer or supplier.

With most financial software and spreadsheets it is possible to run sensitivity analysis or 'what if' scenarios with different inflation rates, prices of fuel etc. and calculate the impact. A hedge against currency fluctuations can be set up if you have any foreign currency transactions.

You may also want to check emergency procedures including disaster management and have a review made of your insurance cover. In most cases there will still be some risk or cost involved since insuring 100% is very expensive or even impossible in some cases.

A contingency amount can be set aside in the budget to be used if something major goes wrong (value should be based on the probability of something occurring multiplied by the expected cost). However, the rules for its use must be clearly defined or you may be tempted to use it to hide over-expenditure. An exceptional marketing campaign, for example, should not qualify unless it is after a major product recall.

Insurance underwriters have statistics for all sorts of disasters, which vary depending on the location and the company's activity (it is more likely that there will be hurricanes in Florida and earthquakes in California than vice versa). If statistics show a 10% chance of a hurricane, take 10% of the likely losses (storm damage including cost of rebuilding and lost business, less the expected insurance payout).

Providing for contingencies is a way of protecting your business by trying to anticipate something going wrong. It is important to keep it as broad as you can. Add all of the identified contingencies to get to the total uninsured risk. This may seem like a lot of work but building a spreadsheet model that can be updated each year will save time.

Calculating the impact of the loss of a major client can be a very important reality check, not only to evaluate your vulnerability, but also the effect on the bottom line and cash flow. Very often a large customer demands high discounts and longer payment terms; they need to be reviewed from time to time to ensure they are still worth doing business with. You need to weigh the loss of future revenue against risk of the outstanding account receivable in case the customer suddenly goes into liquidation. Provisions for Bad Debts should not be overlooked when preparing the budget.

The study of contingencies can result in some benefits via better safety precautions and emergency plans that mitigate losses.

Another important issue is to have a Crises Management Plan in place. In the event of a major problem the whole company should react as one when talking to the Press based on clear policies and procedures set by experts in advance. This is designed to protect the company's image and is more relevant in some activities like pharmaceuticals, but a few years ago a company almost went under as a result of an alleged sexual harassment episode blown out of proportion by the local Press who were quick to print a few conflicting statements.

26 Integration

Have you ever been driving and had to take a detour to avoid road works only to find that there were other road works on the detour?

When you started your business, or when you add a new product or service, you start with an idea (concept). Many people have great ideas but few act upon them and carry them through. Failing to act upon a good idea can be due to lack of confidence, the 'someday syndrome' or lack of a functional plan that materializes the idea and ensures that all parts fit together. Sometimes Entrepreneurs wake up one day, realize they have waited too long and dive in without any preparation.

Many entrepreneurs excel in some, but not all aspects of the business. They may be good with product ideas but not so good with sales. They may be good in sales but struggle with finance.

Even in a concise Business Plan all aspects must be addressed to make sure there are enough resources to produce the desired outcome. By taking command of the whole process, its challenges and the solutions, you will get clear on the course of action and have an integrated view of all that needs to happen and when.

A good Business Plan should be seamless. If the Operational Budget calls for an increase in production beyond the present capacity, then it needs to be linked with the Capital Expenditure Budget (for the funding) and to Human Resources (for the hiring of new staff). Logistics capability also needs to be looked into. If the new machinery will take a certain amount of time to be delivered, installed, tested and staff trained so that it can be running fully, then the extra sales can only occur after this time. If you can't raise finance for the new machinery you will not be able to get the extra production to increase sales unless you outsource it, which would probably change the profitability substantially.

Another example is trying to increase sales in general and at the same time reduce the inventory. Unless there is a new just-in-time system, or an improved system of inventory control, it could be difficult to avoid stock outs and lost or delayed sales. Selling off some old inventory would be an exception, as this should not compromise future sales.

There are some less tangible items that can be difficult to integrate like the Balanced Scorecard Metrics. How long will it take and how much will it cost to raise customer satisfaction by 10%? Different strategies may be required that could either take a long time but cost zero, or be quick but cost a lot.

Regular reviews of the goals, objectives, and interim targets bring everyone back in focus with what they are expected to accomplish. It provides a point of reflection and redirects actions that have strayed. It facilitates proactive management of the chaos, rather than allowing the chaos to manage the company.

27 Buy-In from Partners/Staff

If you are going to hold people accountable for achieving objectives, then you must give them a voice in the preparation of the Business Plan. If objectives are imposed without consultation there may be resentment or indifference where there should have been motivation and a sense of purpose. Everyone needs to feel they have 'skin in the game', that they will gain or lose based on their input to the Plan in addition to their other work.

Each business will have a different approach to involving staff, depending on a variety of factors such as its size, number of staff and hierarchy levels. In any case it is important that a truly sustainable process involves everyone from the very beginning of the planning process through to implementation of agreed actions.

In nearly all businesses there is a great degree of interconnectedness between functions, so it is very important that it is a team buy-in. If a salesman has a potential customer and needs a credit analysis done quickly, so as to reach objectives, it is important that he understands that the Credit and Collection department also has objectives. Selling is vital for the business but there will be a loss if the customer can't pay.

The most senior members of staff from all departments play an important role in ensuring that the plan is realistic and efficient, leverages the overall resources and that there are no inconsistencies or conflicting goals. The objectives must be clearly understood and accepted by everybody so that they feel they own their part and feel motivated and committed to seeing it through.

A Business Plan can help to drive the business and must be integrated into every fiber of an organization, so every employee is contributing towards moving the company in the same direction.

If a department wants to set itself higher objectives, provided there is no conflict with others and their target is achievable, let them. It is a good idea to keep a close watch on how they are doing, just to make sure things don't go wrong. For example, if Logistics think they can handle an increased volume of shipments without increasing staff, hence saving on costs, you should let them do it. However, you need to be sure that there will be no delays in shipping product to customers since this might influence future business and it is 10 times more difficult to get a new customer than to keep a current one satisfied.

If there is a common understanding of how to achieve performance targets, how to out-perform your competition, how to achieve sustainable competitive advantage, how to grow, how to satisfy customers and how to respond to changing market conditions, your whole company will be acting together while strengthening the company's long-term competitive position in the marketplace.

Failure to do this will create a situation similar to a tug-of-war team with five or more ropes. Everybody will be pulling in different directions and not focusing on the main goal. When your company has a clear Plan and takes appropriate action, you get 'traction' to take you from where you are, to where you want to go!

28 Reality Check

> *"Reality is above all else a variable and nobody is qualified to say that he or she knows exactly what it is. As a matter of fact, with a firm enough commitment, you can sometimes create a reality which did not exist before."*
> Margaret Halsey, Novelist

If there is one thing certain in business it is that things change, sometimes literally overnight.

In the past, the commercial environment was not changing anywhere nearly as quickly, so Business Plans were prepared for 3 to 5 year periods with the first year being more detailed.

A thorough Plan must reflect the changing commercial, financial and industrial environment but nowadays changes are taking place at an ever-increasing rate. This means that businesses today have to be much more agile and anticipate the changes in the marketplace as well as the needs of the customers. Furthermore, changes in technology can mean that today's equipment is obsolete tomorrow. Although investors or banks still need medium term projections, it is more realistic for management purposes to put greater effort into short term forecasts. Keep the medium term clear as to the vision, but broad and flexible like a novel that could unfold to more than one ending.

Writing down the direction of the company for the next 90 days helps the leader explain to the team the reasons for decisions about the future so that the whole organization can be in alignment.

To do this you need accurate data as to where you are at the moment and an idea of what the results are likely to be for the next months. For the information on the current situation to be reliable you need to clearly identify any adjustments and exceptional occurrences which impacted the bottom line and distort trends like one-off sales or expenses and indemnities for staff leaving.

The specificities and climate of the company have to be evaluated to ensure that the Plan is realistic and will not be demanding too much from the staff. If everyone has been working very hard to meet the current year's objectives, they may not be physically and mentally capable of higher goals for the next year. A manager with 5 direct reports can't suddenly take care of 5 new hires without making mistakes, leaving important tasks undone or suffer from burn-out. A small company can grow 50% but an established company that has been around for a number of years will probably do very well at 10%.

How is the market? Can you get new customers without lowering prices, offering longer payment terms, improving quality, innovating or incurring higher distribution costs?

Competition usually gets harder, not easier, so it is vital that before incurring additional costs, increasing staff, buying equipment etc. you are very clear on whom your potential new customers are, where you can find them and what exactly they want.

If you didn't have a Business Plan as a starting point you cannot adjust it when the unforeseen happens. You act by trial and error pushed by the events.

The Plan is the basis to work on re-prioritizing or adjusting the variables when faced with a crisis. Set objectives that will be achievable within the time frame you have left. The next task is to work out how you are going to achieve them and have everyone in the organization working in the same direction to make it happen.

29 Reviews and Updates

Unexpected events can occur, for better or worse, that can significantly affect your Business Plan. If you get an unexpected new large customer at the beginning of the year and orders that mean you will exceed the plan, say in month 8, there is no reason why higher objectives should not be set and a brief review of the plan carried out immediately.

On the other hand, if in month 2 you lose a big customer, this should not be a reason for rewriting the plan as this ought to have been considered when you did a 'what if' analysis and the reality check. Management should have designed a contingency plan or, if not, an emergency meeting should take place to come up with a strategy to get to the original target. A change to the plan should only be made if there is little chance of getting back on track.

The reason for this duality in criteria is that when you plan, you are realistic but on the conservative side. If you are clearly doing much better and it wasn't just a timing issue, you should adjust your planning.

If you do worse you have a responsibility to all stakeholders to come up with strategies to overcome the downturn.

The Plan and especially the Budget are not set in concrete. However, reworking them can be time consuming and may cause errors, so it should only be done for significant events. Depending upon the size and type of business it might be more efficient and effective to forecast the quarterly or annual results and treat these as the new objectives.

When staff knows that the Budget is unachievable due to circumstances outside their control, shifting the effort towards achieving the forecast may keep them motivated instead of having an unrealistic target to strive for.

Another example would be if a fire was to break out in your offices (God forbid). This event could cause months of chaos. In this case it might be better to make a plan for getting the office operational again which would replace the Business Plan until this objective is achieved.

Because of market or economic conditions you may need to adjust your features or services, change the pricing or your distribution strategies, alter your staffing plans, widen or narrow your target market or even fundamentally change your product or service. In the long run, you have to keep your focus on the goals.

To be successful and surpass any obstacles be flexible in the tactics (short term) but firm in the strategy (medium/long term). There are times that you need to bend in order not to break.

The most successful Entrepreneurs are not necessarily those who write the best Business Plans to start with. The best are those who are good at listening to their customers, who have the intuition to predict market changes and who lead a well-oiled team where everyone is accountable, so that adjustments to the business are implemented quickly and appropriately.

30 Putting it Into Action

It is a common mistake to think that Business Plans or Budgets are just financial exercises to obtain financing or for the accountants to worry about. But this is not the case. They are much more than that – they are commercial and strategic documents dealing with the business's goals and objectives.

The Business Plan depends very much on the human elements around it, from the elaboration process, through the commitment and involvement to the tracking and follow-up that comes afterwards.

If an adverse event occurs between finalizing the Plan and the start of the new period there is often a tendency towards 'business as usual' while the Plan is being fully revised. This can take several weeks, and at the end of this period the objectives set are no longer realistic or achievable because the company has drifted in the wrong direction.

If this was to occur, a 90 days Emergency Plan should be designed on the fly because it is better to work with a poor plan than with no plan. This contingency plan, focusing only on what is most relevant, should be closely monitored by management and clearly communicated to all the staff. This would allow the necessary time to adjust the more detailed Plan.

Another frequent reaction to adverse events is to freeze expenditure, particularly hiring, training and travel. If the hiring, training and travel were in the budget then they should be expenses that are necessary for the proper functioning of the business, staff motivation and achieving the revenue goals. Any changes to the plan should be evaluated even when time constraints are an issue.

The annual Operations Budget is normally incorporated into monthly or quarterly reports where the actual results are compared with the budget and variations analyzed. If the budget isn't broken down by department or cost center it will be impossible to hold people accountable for the results.

Depending on the number of departments, locations and cost centers this can result in a large quantity of data that can get out of hand if not properly coordinated. Always be aware of the cost/benefit analysis. When does too much detail become counterproductive? What are the key numbers that have to be monitored in greater detail?

Less is usually more – once you have the essentials covered, flexibility trumps detail.

Although the Business Plan should not go into too much detail, each Department must translate its guidelines into clear workable steps. For instance, the Sales Department has to break objectives by product into weekly targets so that an order pipeline is developed with a certain number of phone calls to prospects, follow-ups and visits. If this work isn't done well there can be a lack of coordination with production, purchasing and logistics. If the breakdown is not true to the Plan the margins may be reduced or the strategic moves into different markets or segments won't happen and the Plan will not be put into action.

Timing is also crucial. If you fall behind what is planned, don't start inventing new solutions. While success is never guaranteed, your chances of success will be better if you stick to the plan that was put together taking into consideration all market and internal considerations known at the time.

Main Takeaways:

1.

2.

3.

Improvements to implement:

Action 1.

By: Start Date: Ready by:

Action 2.

By: Start Date: Ready by:

Action 3.

By: Start Date: Ready by:

Product and Marketing Strategy

Think about your industry, the present outlook and the future possibilities.

What is your product or service, who do you sell to, how is the product or service distributed and what are the new products or services and industry developments that will benefit or adversely affect your business?

What are the unique features in your product or service?

Which factors make it successful?

The high quality of your products or services, the location, your customer support, the money back guaranty, or your state-of-the-art equipment?

In **www.BusinessGrowthLevers.com/resources** you will find tools to develop the Marketing Strategy in your business.

31 Create First and Sell Later

'Build it and they will come' has become a pre-historic concept.

If you have done your market research and niche identification, you should know your market(s). You should be able to describe for each product or service you sell the typical customers who will buy it. Are they male, female, between what ages, what income, where do they live, what are their hobbies, where do they hang out, what do they look like, what other products and services do they consume?

If it seems strange that you should know all this about the buyers of each of your products or services, let me ask you two questions:

1) If you don't, how do you communicate with them? How do you craft the right message?

2) How did you create the product or service in the first place?

The exception is, of course if you sell commodities. If your company sells rice, for instance, you don't have to know all that about your customer because when it gets to the moment of buying, chances are the prevailing factor will be the price. The same goes for many other commodities although in some cases they may have different products for different profiles.

The next question would be - does your product have to stay a commodity or can you transform it into an experience? That is what Starbucks has done with coffee…

If you are still working in the old paradigm of manufacturing or buying the product and then use marketing and sales to get the potential customers to buy it, beware of the changes in the buying process. Customers have more choices, are better informed and hold more power than ever!

Having a good product or service is not enough. If you are the best kept secret in your business nobody will buy. However, massive advertising campaigns are too expensive and the 'noise' is so loud with everybody using the same media that the consumers have learnt to 'switch off' from all the advertising that is constantly bombarding them in every shape and form everywhere they go.

'Product centric marketing', focused on the product or service and its features, with a message to the masses, has long been replaced by 'customer orientated marketing', focused on differentiation and in providing not just features but emotions and a one to one relationship.

If you haven't made this shift, it is a miracle that you are still in business! Rethink your strategy and consider 'value driven marketing', focused on values - produced locally, environment friendly - and based on functionalities, emotions, spirit of collaboration and fairness.

We live in an age of globalization where we all need to participate more actively in doing what is right for the environment and social sustainability – our survival is on the line.

"Tell me and I'll forget; show me and I may remember; involve me and I'll understand"
Chinese Proverb

32 Lack of Research

Successful product creation is not easy. Technology and markets are changing continuously and the speed of change is increasing every day.

Competition in most industries is on a high (with price cuts and discounts) and customer loyalty at a low... The monumental changes that constantly impact commerce have forced companies to innovate with increasing speed, efficiency, and quality. This has made new product development one of the most complex and difficult business functions. However, firms must innovate in order to survive.

One of the principle tools you need to use before you launch a product or service in any stage of your company's life is market research, to be aware of the trends in the industry, your consumer's preferences and your competition. Studying your market gives you a better understanding not only of the potential for profit, but also of what those who would purchase your product are demanding in terms of features, reliability and performance.

To be able to undertake strategic product creation you need to identify which market niche will be most responsive to your product and perform tests with consumers corresponding to the right profile as well as laboratory tests for safety and durability (if it is a physical product).

Through surveys, literature research, internet research and other information gathering techniques, you can learn individual preferences of your potential customers and identify the trends.

If you are in a well-defined industry, like footwear manufacturing, you might find that your professional organization has already collected important data. If not, you just need to gather it yourself or ask for professional help.

Market research is imperative because we all have different tastes and ideas about what's important in our lives as well as different perceptions on the price we are willing to pay for the goods or services we need or want to buy.

Small business owners often think they have a great idea for a new product or service, only to discover that either people are not willing to pay the price that the business needs to charge to make a profit or that they don't want that service or product at all. Even if they are lucky and the market accepts the new product or service, research will allow them to introduce small improvements or other new products and services that would work well with the new idea, allowing the small business owner to see future growth into new areas.

Market research will also reveal the strengths and weaknesses of the existing products and services and give you the opportunity to better serve the market.

Information on prices and distribution channels will also be invaluable when designing your product. Finding out what your customers want and what they are willing to pay saves time and ensures you launch the right product or service to the market at the right price point.

Product testing will also provide you with tips for your marketing plan by highlighting the products or services' benefits and strengths.

Don't be afraid to dip your toe into the market with real products on a test basis if the market research is not conclusive. It is better to make mistakes on a small scale and have the opportunity to course correct than to go head first, full scale and miss the mark!

33 Knowing Your Competition

In order to be successful it is imperative that business owners know their market – not just the consumers (customers and/or potential customers) but, very important, the competition – the products and services they are providing, their market share, how aggressive they are, their reputation, etc.

In a competitive business environment, understanding who you are competing against is one of the best strategies business owners can use to advance their marketing activities.

Identify your competition and learn everything that you can about their businesses, products and services. Make it a priority to always be up to date with what they are doing and on the look-out for any other new arrivals in the market either for similar products or for products that fulfil similar needs. Keep an eye on the media and in your industry's independent newsletters, blogs and Social Media.

Getting information about your competitors can give you the leading edge, as it can show you ways in which your company can be unique in fulfilling existent or emerging consumer needs or preferences.

The best way to know your competition is to become a customer yourself, not just pretend that you are interested. Ask lots of questions and test their ability to serve you. Take note of their pricing, their offering and their distribution and delivery models to compare to your own business. You can gain great competitive intelligence by simply stepping into their customer's shoes.

Talk to your competitors' customers. Ask them why they prefer those products or services. Get them to be specific.

Is it the quality of the product or service, the price, the location, or the customer support?

Is there something they don't like? Why? How could it be better?

Visit their websites and analyse how they position themselves, how they offer their products or services and what key differentiators they promote. Some websites list company events, client testimonials and other valuable information that will provide you with insight.

Find out everything you can about who is running your competitor's business. Attend industry conferences and trade shows even if you are not an exhibitor. Visit your competitors' booths, familiarize yourself with their product or service offerings and strategies; listen to their sales people and to the visitors' comments. Take the opportunity to meet them personally. This will give you a better understanding of who they are and help you to anticipate their moves.

If a competitor is trying to increase his market share, he might lower his prices; if he wants to launch a new product or service he may kick off a marketing campaign. Knowing this in time will allow you to study response scenarios and hold your position in the marketplace.

If you feel uncomfortable about these suggestions remember that your competitors are also doing it and as long as you do it openly and with integrity the only consequence is a better service to the client. How? If all players in each market are constantly trying to provide a better service to the consumers the overall quality will increase and innovation will continuously be stimulated.

One final word, knowing your competitors doesn't mean you should be copying them. You need to stand out, not just be one of the herd. Remember that keeping the consumers happy is the main objective of any business!

34 Knowing Why You are Different

Being able to identify and promote key differentiators for your products and services is imperative for your company's survival. If the customers don't perceive this difference and value it, your products or services will be amongst all the others who compete based just on price. And that is a fight where everybody loses, including the clients because they lose on quality and service.

If you are the best in something you don't need to compete provided you have crafted a unique value proposition that is perceived to have real value by your current and potential customers. Price stops being an issue because you have managed to connect emotionally with your clients and provide them with an experience instead of a pack of features. This is the sweet spot all business should strive to find.

If you already have a reasonable number of clients, ask them why they buy your product or service and why they think it is better than the competition. The answers may come as a surprise to you but they are the foundation to your differentiation and the core of your brand. They should also be the core of your marketing campaigns. Use your clients' exact words since they are the ones that resonate best with your niche.

It is better to connect strongly with a niche than be one amongst many for the masses. Once you have become leader in your market you can always go after other niches with the necessary adjustments in the product or service and the message.

Another way of adjusting to the market requirements is to promote internal brainstorming sessions with your team and ask them what is the one specific attribute, characteristic or differentiator that sets your product or service apart from your competition. Sales departments and Customer Services are in regular contact with the customers and hence have an invaluable perception of the clients' needs and opinions.

Ask your staff to make a list of your competitors and their promise or position in the market. Most likely they come from different backgrounds and if they also ask for their friends and family's opinions you will get input from a large spectrum of consumers.

What is the first thing that comes to mind when you think of product X (from a competitor)?

Do the clients value that aspect?

Do you offer the same features and results?

Do your customers know it?

Identify the attributes your products or services possess that are different from your competition and evaluate which are the ones that your customers find most desirable. Once you have identified the most important one you will have your Differential Claim.

Your USP (Unique Selling Proposition) needs to be so compelling for your target market that they pre-qualify themselves to buy your product or service. It usually fulfills a need that is not met by your competitors, which they fail to communicate or that is not perceived by consumers.

Look for these performance gaps, know your market, your product or service and the value and results customers get when they buy it. Be creative. Make small adjustments that will add unique perceived value or provide guarantees. Offer proof; don't expect your future customers to take your word for it.

Remember that the buying decision for non-commodities is based mainly on emotion. Create an experience and involve your clients by constantly interacting with them. Make them feel part of a community, be consistent and always deliver on your promises. In fact, over-deliver consistently and you have a good chance of having clients for life!

35 Building a Brand

When customers hear your business name, what do you think comes to their mind?

What is the lasting impression?

A brand is more than a trademark, name or symbol used to identify a company... it is the emotional connection with your customers and the perception they have of experiencing your products or services.

A brand is not something you build on its own. It is the by-product of the experience you provide consistently to your customers. It is your identity and a reflection of your company's values. Once built, it is a powerful asset that will connect you with customers and that will act as a guarantee every time you launch other products or services.

The goal of every business owner is not just to create satisfied customers but to turn the customers into raving fans. In today's market, word of mouth and Social Media play such an important role that a company's brand is controlled largely by the consumers and can be supported or destroyed with a few clicks of the mouse.

Think about products you use in your everyday life. Do you reach for a tissue or a Kleenex? When you tell someone to research something, do you say "Google it"?

The Brits often 'hoover' their carpets... The Americans 'Xerox' their documents... We all use 'post it' (3M brand) rather than 'repositionable notes' ('sticky notes' was a trademark of Bic that didn't stick).

These are real examples of successful branding.

Create an authentic brand promise, the essence of what your company stands for and what you tell your customers they can expect from you each and every time they come in contact with your company. The best way to build a brand is to stay true to your original purpose and passion instead of trying to adopt an artificial 'persona' that doesn't feel authentic and trustworthy to your customers. A brand promise has to be unique, compelling and believable. What guarantees can you offer in the form of a brand promise? Could it be customized solutions? Do you offer the cheapest price?... the highest quality?... the fastest delivery? What does your brand stand for?

Create a real brand culture in your company by making sure that every single person understands and acts according to the brand promise. Are you delivering on your brand promise each and every time a customer or potential client is experiencing your organization?

Focus on every single element that touches your customer, the market or potential customers - it could be your staff and their behaviors, your internal systems (technology, invoices, phone, website, etc.) or your external systems (your products or services, the way they are delivered, your marketing or your Customer Service).

Success is a combination of factors where leadership, a strong promise, exceptional service and compelling message play an important role. The strength of the brand reflects the company's reputation and, if damaged, can compromise its survival.

36 Believing in the Power of Marketing

Many times small business owners place a few adverts, participate in a trade show or do a direct mail campaign and because the response is weak they start questioning the power of marketing.

Marketing has evolved to include building customer relationships as well as the traditional 4 P's.

Product - developing the products or services that customers want.

Price - pricing the products or services adequately.

Placement - making them readily available to the customers.

Promotion - developing and implementing a strategy that not only convinces customers that the product or service is preferable to its competition, but that it is clearly the only real choice.

Marketing is based on the principle that profitable sales and satisfactory returns on investment can only be achieved by identifying, anticipating and satisfying customer needs and desires, thus making selling easier. Is it relevant for your business to use psychology, sociology, anthropology and neuroscience like some Fortune 500 corporations? Yes, although obviously not to the same extent and levels of investment.

Any company who wants to serve its customers and be successful needs to make sure there is a market for its products or services. It must gather information from surveys, clients, suppliers and competitors, population statistics and industry data before setting realistic goals and finding the best way to reach those goals.

You may be doing some of this without realizing it because your experience and intuition guide you. As your company grows and with the market becoming increasingly competitive there is less and less margin for making mistakes, so it is essential to have a consistent and well-targeted marketing plan and to follow it. No matter how amazing, appealing or unique your product or service is, if it is marketed to the wrong people in the wrong way it will never reach its full potential.

One of the biggest mistakes you can make is to try to be 'all things to all people'. Focusing on a few niches or target markets you will be far more successful. Don't be frightened to limit the number of prospects you specifically target. Less is more. Even the best products in the world won't be a success if they aren't marketed with the most appealing message to the intended market.

Unless your product or service is a commodity, people won't buy it because of what is does (features), but because of the results it will bring to them (benefits). If you incorporate personality and innovative marketing approaches that grab attention and remove as many risks as you can from the buying process by offering guarantees, you will attract the right prospects to your sales funnel.

Remember people will buy when the moment is right for them! Statistics say that only 7% of people are ready to buy most products or services (again I'm not talking about everyday commodities). You need to constantly reach out and educate them, give them a reason to get involved in your 'community' to eventually get more enquires and sales.

If people develop the 'like and trust' factor with your company's brand and you keep them engaged, you will stay at the top of their minds and will be chosen when the buying decision is made. More than that, if the product or service satisfies them, they are likely to recommend you and buy again from you in the future.

37 Inconsistent Message or Unrealistic Marketing Plan

> *'We're in one of those great historical periods that occur every 200 to 300 years when people don't understand the world anymore, when the past is not sufficient to explain the future'.*
> Peter Drucker (writer, consultant and teacher)

A common mistake Entrepreneurs make is to send out mixed or inconsistent messages to their market. Most often this is due to inexperience in marketing and not being clear about the target or the brand promise. Other times they think that doing what the competition does is a good strategy.

You need to create a unique identity and back it up with a series of messages and images that support your brand. Every point that touches your customer or potential customer – logo, packaging (if it applies),

TV, radio or press advertising, billboards, flyers, internet, etc. must support the brand image you are trying to convey. Your language and words must be coherent and your service delivery, response time and product must support your brand message.

Repetition is the key in marketing and your potential customers need to see your name, brand and image over and over and over again before it registers that you are there. Customers have short attention spans and poor memories, except when something really catches their attention and speaks to their hearts.

A bad Marketing Plan is one that doesn't get your message to the best potential customers while an unrealistic plan might reach the right audience but with insufficient impact. Both can be costly and a waste of money. The critical factor is to know who your potential customers are and determining the most cost effective way to reach them.

If you have been working without a plan, getting new clients has just been a fortunate accident.

General distrust of advertising and constant proliferation of multiply forms of promotion results in very few people reacting until they have been 'exposed' to a product or service a number of times. It used to be an average of 7 points of contact before a buyer felt confident to do business with a seller, but now is thought to be 11. Marketing Plans need to be strategic, creative and diversified so that people become familiar with the product or service and come to know, like and trust it.

In the last decade newspaper circulation has fallen, post boxes are crammed with fliers, recording or downloading TV programs means you can fast forward instead of zapping to avoid adverts, all of which make it harder to reach your target via traditional methods. Within the Internet platforms are coming and going with frequent changes in advertising rules. Testing has to be an integral part of your marketing. This is not only to distinguish between what works and what doesn't but also to fine-tune what works and determine what works the best.

Sending students out into the streets to check responses is fine for products like toothpaste, but is irrelevant for non-consumer goods.

You need to determine the best advertising and promotion strategy to support your objective. This includes a description of the marketing material as well as a schedule of planned promotional activities such as special sales, coupons, contests and events.

Online marketing is getting to be the most used marketing system, since it is inexpensive in terms of cost to reach the target audience. However, the low cost should be no excuse for not keeping it extremely targeted and consistent or it will lose its effectiveness.

38 Wrong Positioning and/or Pricing

Product positioning is a crucial decision that the business owner (or the management team) needs to make and implement in order to establish a distinctive and strong image of their product or service in the minds of the target consumers. Very often a product fails because of wrong positioning or inability to convey the unique attributes that set it apart from the competition.

The more innovative and remarkable your product or service is, the higher you can position and price it, since the benefits are unlike those offered by the competition and its unique components add perceived value to customers. Adding a chapter to an e-book is not necessarily adding value, but adding a list of free resources for readers is.

What are you selling to whom?

What is distinctive about your products or services that will be hard for your competitors to reproduce?

What is the perceived value of that difference to the potential customers?

Technology, design, high quality, reliability and exceptional customer service can be distinctive factors that bring sustainable value vs. the competition if, and only if, the customer perceives it that way. The key issue will then be finding people who will pay more for that value, and then crafting the right message and the right way to reach them.

Positioning is thus all about finding the right path to create a significant and unique place amidst a crowd of different competing brands.

How big is the segment?

How are you going to reach them?

How will you communicate the reasons to buy your products or services over the competition?

People cannot make decisions balancing more than two to four differentiating factors at a time. If there are more, they will get lost. If you can identify one thing that really makes the difference in the perceived value, stick to it. Your marketing message will be clearer.

If you already have a strong brand, you can position a new product or service at a higher level and ask for a higher price. However, this initial advantage won't protect you from failure if the customer buys the product or service and the perceived value fails to meet his or her expectations. In extreme situations, your other products or services may suffer because the brand loyalty is broken and the customers may start questioning if their perception was accurate.

If customers see your product or service as a commodity your salespeople will have to battle constant price objections. Focus your effort in constantly improving the value that is perceived by your customers. This includes, but is not limited to packaging, design, attitude of your sales force, advertising, web site, interactions with customers in your products' Social Media pages, response to customers' recommendations, quality of customers' support and your company and products or services' reputation and pricing.

Pricing strategy can be complex, but some basic rules should be followed so that it doesn't undermine the success of the business – all prices must cover costs plus a margin, they should reflect the dynamics of cost, demand, competition and preserve balance in the marketplace.

Price wars are a disservice for the clients and may have little impact on sales while ruining the margins. Evaluate your exposure to changes in the market so that you have the appropriate response already outlined.

39 Too Much Competition

Businesses exist in a competitive environment. Supermarkets are in fierce competition with each other to provide the most suitable range of products at the best price. Businesses compete in many ways, price being one of the most common, but there are other ways to gain market advantage like customization, speed and comfort of delivery, location, customer service, hassle free purchasing, guarantees, etc.

Quality and differentiation are usually powerful weapons against direct competitors (who provide similar products or services) as well as indirect ones (different products or services that could be an alternative for the same niche and similar level of expenditure).

Do you think you have too much competition? Make a list of the companies (products and services) that compete in your target market. There are bound to be aspects in which their businesses and products are different from yours. This might help you to identify differentiating factors - price, quality, product warranty, speed of repair, etc.

It is important to study your competition and their strategy, to know their strengths and weaknesses. Learn from their successes but above all from their mistakes. The knowledge of your competition will provide you with information for developing sound strategies to outperform them. Suddenly a niche or a marketing angle might appear and you could find it easier to get clients.

Competitors are a positive influence in the market. They raise customer awareness to the need for that type of product or service. That's where you come in with a more customized solution and higher perceived value. Decide to be a leader in your niche market. By targeting smaller markets where you can make more of a difference you avoid competing with larger companies.

Niching achieves high margins, which enables your business to grow rapidly. Fierce competition, even within your niche, will push you to continuously innovate but be careful not to focus too much on the competition or your business will become too reactive. You need to formulate and execute a consistent, customer centered, strategy and move towards your goals.

Research constantly what your potential customers are passionate about, what they value the most, and give them more of it. Interact with them and listen with attention to what they say. This will allow you to identify new opportunities and emerging needs as well as which customer groups are the most important to serve given your resources and objectives. This is the key to long term profits.

Ponder if any of your 'competitors' are really potential joint-venture partners. Some customers would be better served with their products and vice versa so if you joined efforts there would be a win-win for both businesses. Perhaps you are at full capacity or the customer is located in an area that is too far for you to deliver to economically. It is better to suggest a competitor you trust than just say you can't take the order. You could gain by either getting a commission or reciprocal business and you will be improving customer satisfaction.

40 Don't Know Your Customers

'Your most unhappy customers are your greatest source of learning'
Bill Gates (founder of Microsoft)

Product and Marketing Strategy

Who are your customers and what, and why, do they buy from you?

This information is critical if you want to grow, since it relates to actual buyers, not hypothetical marketing data on potential customers. Even where a market study is made by experienced professionals there can often be misleading data due to lack of response or untrue statements. What better source of data than your actual, real customers? Better still is to know why you have lost a customer so you can take corrective action where needed.

Let's dig a little deeper into whom your customers are.

If you sell to businesses, is it just to one industry or are clients spread over many?

Are there any unusual customers that might point to a niche market that can be developed?

The same with the geographic location of customers - where are you already strong and why?

Which is the most critical, delivery time or delivery cost?

Next, break down the type of products that customers buy, again by industry and geography.

Are there customers who buy only one type when you should be selling them several?

What are they using the products for? Perhaps they have some new use for them that you should know about and be developing. Perhaps they could use an additional service that you can provide without much investment or change in your current operations.

Where did you get your customers from in the first place?

This is important because it shows which channels have worked best in the past. Since trends change over time, the more recently acquired clients are the best indicator of where you can get new customers. For example, Trade Fairs are exceptionally good in some industries and exceptionally bad in others - they may provide a lot of contacts, but how many actually turn into customers?

A well implemented CRM (Customer Relationship Management) system can provide a lot of very useful information, if it is easy to use.

How much of your business is repeat sales?

How many of your customers come through referrals?

How much does it cost to acquire a new customer?

Relationships need to be developed with customers so that not only their current needs are known but also their probable future requirements. To get them to tell you their plans you will have to build trust and show that you are there to help them solve their problems, not just get extra business for yourself.

This is a medium/long term task, but it can be broken down into key customers by major markets. Each key customer should know where their market is headed and be in a place to give you information that will be useful to anticipate their needs and the needs for other companies in the same market.

Main Takeaways:

1.

2.

3.

Improvements to implement:

Action 1.

By: Start Date: Ready by:

Action 2.

By: Start Date: Ready by:

Action 3.

By: Start Date: Ready by:

Sales

A lot of entrepreneurs are not clear on the distinction between Marketing and Sales.

Marketing is everything that you do to reach and persuade prospects. It is a planning and positioning function. Without it you would not have prospects or leads to follow up with.

The Sales process is everything that you do to close the sale after the prospect is identified. The ultimate goal is to get a signed agreement or contract, but it can result in pointing the client to another solution or another moment in time if this is what serves the client best. It is a system, a process based on interpersonal interaction. Without good sales techniques the closing rate might hold back the business.

With a physical shop the Marketing is about educating, informing and enticing the potential customers so that they enter the shop ready to look at the merchandise. The Selling will be the interaction that takes place in the shop between the people and the staff until a satisfied customer leaves the premises.

By strategically combining the efforts of both Marketing and Sales there is a much greater likelihood of successful business growth.

In **www.BusinessGrowthLevers.com/resources** you will find tips on how to sell more effectively.

41 Systematized Sales Structure

No matter what you are selling, every sale includes in one form or another some steps that a salesperson needs to master to be able to thrive. A user friendly, but complete tracking system covering all the phases is indispensable for evaluating results and linking to the other departments in the company.

Sales training is a good investment especially if it is backed up with coaching and mentoring from experienced salespeople. No company can afford to have their revenue generating frontline run wild. It is a big mistake to hire people, even with experience in sales, and after some basic training on the product or service turn them loose! It is imperative that they learn your company's system, since it should weigh 95% in their approach to customers, leaving only 5% to personal style. Potential clients may empathize more with salesperson A or B but the methodology and message used in the process should be identical in its essence.

Regular sales team meetings will help keeping the team synchronized and motivated. The niche and client's profile, strategic priorities and approach need to be clearly communicated to the sales force.

Salespeople can prepare a sales letter, try going door-to-door, attend events in chambers of commerce and local associations or join sports clubs or gyms for personal, informal interaction. Another option is to go for online sales through paid adverts and Social Media. Choice depends on the product or service's characteristics and target market.

After the first contact is established and the potential customer has been pre-qualified it is important to have a formal meeting with the decision maker. This meeting should be presented as informational, providing some value to the prospect.

Sales people must keep up to speed with the trends and what is happening in the market so that the clients are interested in talking to them. It is also important that the prospects know how long the meeting will take – saying it will take 10 minutes and then holding them hostages for an hour is the wrong approach to making a future sale. If the prospect (decision maker) is not available for the period of time that is needed, the meeting should be rescheduled.

First impressions are critical – the salesperson should offer some valuable smoking hot information about the market or industry, make the prospect laugh or whatever is appropriate to create empathy. Then, the salesperson should ask open questions to invite the sharing of information and show respect and heart felt interest in the prospect's problems. Only after enough information has been gathered should the salesperson suggest one or two ways your company's product or service could solve or improve the issues.

Presentations should be tailored to fit each prospect (it is part of the preparation work to collect personal information about them). This will show real commitment in helping their company, add credibility and build empathy if well done.

The salesperson should be prepared to deal with objections, but the best approach it to anticipate potential issues and address them during the presentation. All meetings should finish with 'next action steps'.

Once all questions have been answered via meetings, e-mails or phone, the salesperson should ask for the sale – "Is there any reason why we can't start working together next week?" If the potential client says "Yes", he will have to give a justification, the objection can be addressed and the question asked again!

Last, but not least, always ask for referrals. If it is the wrong timing or fit but the salesperson has done a good job the prospect will be happy to recommend someone else. If the prospect becomes a customer, then he will be in a position to give you a referral and a testimonial!

42 Prospect Qualification

The potential clients' profiling and niching used for marketing is the guideline for the sales people to find the prospects.

Let's say you have determined that your ideal client is married, in his mid-thirties, has an annual income of $100,000 or more, owns his home and has an executive-level job. Now you can start thinking about where you would find such a person (your marketing department may have that information already).

Communication between departments is, as always, very important and a two way street. Marketing identifies the niche and profile and sales provide feedback on what prospects and clients need and want. This precious information should be systematized in all sales meetings.

Finding potential prospects is a critical phase in a salesperson's work. According to a survey, there are usually 10 out of 100 prospects that are qualified to purchase. Of those 10, there are probably only 3 who have the immediate need to buy. So how do you find those 3 buyers?

Finding the right prospects is the key to selling, but knowing how to qualify your prospects is the key to selling successfully. For example, if you sell top quality toothpaste, one obvious source for this market would be the dentists in your area. If you give them samples of your product, they will give them to their patients and that adds to the credibility of your product.

Success in qualifying prospects comes from asking enough right questions, in the right places, to the right people.

Who has the most urgent need for the products or services?

Who has the most obvious need?

Who has the money?

Who has influence over the prospects they were able to identify?

It is important to write down in detail the ideal prospects identified.

Where do the ideal prospects live, work, socialize, worship or play?

Where can sales staff find directories from which they can form their own lists?

Where could they go and meet new prospects?

Priorities should be set up by using 'why' and 'what' questions:

Why would the prospects be likely to buy the product or service?

Why would they resist buying?

Why might this be a good (or bad) time to approach the prospects?

What will the prospects find most beneficial about the product or service?

What information should be gathered about the prospects before meeting with them?

What questions should be asked to get prospects to talk about their needs?

When is the best time to contact the prospects?

When are prospects most likely to be available for meetings?

How can prospecting and qualifying skills be improved?

After finding qualified prospects for the product or service, sales people must establish if the prospects have the authority to buy and the ability to pay.

In the first meeting and before both parties' time is wasted, it is imperative that confirmation is obtained that the people involved are both able and potentially willing to make the purchase. Time is a precious resource and without the presence of the person who has the authority to make a decision on the sale there is no point going beyond the stage of primary information gathering.

Be upfront, polite but firm and reschedule the meeting.

43 Knowing How to Deal with Sales Objections

Good salespeople need to know about their product or service, about the prospect (hence the importance of preparation and previous research) and about themselves. Self-knowledge is an essential factor - specially the awareness of their own triggers so they can play to their strengths and avoid their weaknesses.

The combination of technique with honesty, conviction and a positive attitude will help prospects to resolve any lingering doubts or conflict. No matter how excellent the product or service is, prospects will always raise objections. The salespeople's success depends on their ability to anticipate and handle them.

So how do you handle objections?

The first step is to come across as a knowledgeable, interested person whose mission is to help the clients achieve their objectives.

The main reasons for objections are skepticism, misunderstanding, bad timing or lack of interest altogether. The last two should be uncovered as soon as possible and the meeting postponed or ended.

Skepticism and misunderstanding may arise from failure to establish rapport, lack of preparation for the meeting, not asking the right questions or listen actively to the client's answers. Intelligent questions both explore the prospect's needs and surface possible objections so that these can be eliminated as the conversation flows. Giving clear and confident answers to any questions is also paramount. It is better to say you don't know (but you will find out) then to be vague.

Discuss benefits more than features. Provide specific examples of how the prospect will benefit from the product or service. If the prospect seems to be stalling, ascertain whether the timing is wrong and if that is the case, move on.

An exercise to help deal with objections is to review your presentation in detail with the purpose of identifying as many possible objections as you can and practice different answers. If the client says "Your price is too high"… don't take it personally and explain without being defensive why prices are higher than the competition or just ask…"when compared to what?" Sometimes you can turn the objection into a reason for buying, like "that solution has far more capacity than I need now"…"well Mr. X, one more reason for you to buy, because it will allow your company to grow without further investment!" If you can do this, the client won't be able to use that objection again.

If you feel the client has some reason for not buying the product or service that he hasn't stated yet, ask him what it is. Address the issue and ask him again if there is any other reason why he wouldn't make the purchase. Only by narrowing the objections down to one objection and then asking "If I could solve that issue for you would you place the order?" you can identify the real issues. Otherwise, you waste time and don't know exactly why he is not buying.

Remember these golden rules: never argue, contradict or be sarcastic with a client and never make it personal! It is all about the product or service and you want to help the client. Never assume you know what he means. Clarify any terms he uses that are vague or unclear. Never lie. If a feature is missing or has poor performance acknowledge and reinforce the compensating factors and strong points. If the client complains about a past experience with your company show surprise, apologize and guarantee it won't happen again. Never blame another department and, of course do not badmouth the competition.

When you are overcoming objections don't dwell too long on any single objection because you will amplify its importance in the mind of your prospect. Your answers should be just long enough to satisfy the potential customer. Use testimonials, past experiences or whatever relevant information you have.

Objections are a way of finding out exactly what the client's needs really are, what he fears and what he is not prepared to accept. The quicker the objections are uncovered and dealt with the more chances you have of closing the sale.

44 Wrong Perspective on Closing

The 'close' of the sale is usually described as the point where a prospect or customer agrees to buy.

Many times, salespeople separate the sales presentation from the close. This happens because they fear the moment when they are going to have to wrestle the prospect for a decision, and more often than not, they get a "No". Buyers are equally negative about the second phase and determined not to be 'closed'.

Salespeople who respect their customers believe they are intelligent individuals with whom they wish to have a long-term and mutually beneficial relationship, so the primary goal is to provide them with products and services that will make them successful, not to sell anything just for the sake of making a sale! The objective is to create a win-win long term business relationship.

In today's tough economic environment and global competition buyers are more cautious about buying, so the sales process is often longer and more difficult. At each interaction with the prospects the salespeople will be achieving deeper mutual understanding and establishing clarity about the process. They have a direction and understand where the meeting needs to go in order to maintain momentum and win the deal.

Every step along the way represents a stage of a decision path which, if managed correctly, will lead to a satisfactory outcome.

Listening very carefully to what prospects are saying will give salespeople signals as to how to create a win-win situation and also on how to maximize the prospects' awareness of their dissatisfaction with the present situation. Asking open-ended, non-leading checking questions allows them to gauge how the prospects are responding so they adjust the solution accordingly.

It is important to evaluate honestly whether the prospects' dissatisfaction supports the need for a customized solution or not. It is a mistake to close a sale that would, in the long run, alienate the customer and damage the relationship or the company's reputation.

Prospects and customers will have more respect for salespeople who are truthful about whether their products or services can help to solve their problems. Credibility is very important for repeat business. One sale lost now can mean several sales and referrals in the future.

It is important to help clients see a clear picture of the desired outcome and expectations. Give the prospects a concise, powerful summary that reiterates the benefits of your products or services. Once you've done this, make one final check to give them the opportunity to make any final objections that might interfere with your close. If another objection surfaces, handle it, and then restate the final check.

Be direct and ask for the business confidently and clearly. Regardless of whether you made the sale or not, end the meeting with energy, and rapport to make a positive last impression. Thank the client for their time and reinforce your desire to work with them in the future.

If the customer commits to the sale it is the beginning of a new phase that is as important (if not more so) as the sales process - the delivery of the product or service and follow-up to assure the customer's success in executing the purchased solution.

Salespeople should always follow up with customers whether they close the sale or not. The most successful sales people are the ones who have repeat business or that keep close and genuine interest in qualified prospects so that they turn them into customers in the future.

45 Over Focus on New Customers

Have you been along to your bank and seen they are offering gifts, special rates or no bank charges for new customers? Did that make you feel that you should be changing banks because they treat new customers better than existing ones?

Statistically it is seven times easier to maintain an existing client than to go out and get a new one. However, many business owners are obsessed with trying to find new customers, making sure the advertising, displays and pricing all 'scream out' to attract new buyers.

If human nature was not so adverse to change there would be even more customers changing suppliers, but remember that those who stay just due to inertia are no longer likely to recommend the product or service to others.

The focus on pursuing new customers is certainly prudent and necessary, but it should be only one part of the equation. Business owners should also dedicate a lot of attention and time to existing clients with special focus on two groups: the 20 percent who are currently their best customers and the clients with best growth potential. In the present economic conditions it would probably be wise to add a third group: those who always pay on time...

Building customer loyalty is a big challenge but it usually pays. Studies have shown that in most businesses loyal customers represent about 20 percent of the customer base, but make up more than 50 percent of the revenue from sales.

Existing customers often phone or e-mail you and tell you what they want so that no selling is needed. Their details, address, tax number etc. are already on file along with credit rating and their payments history so that less time and effort is needed. Communication with these customers on a regular basis in person, by telephone and email makes them feel appreciated, provides you with valuable information on their needs and on how to keep on serving them with excellence.

The knowledge you have of your existing customers will also provide you with opportunities when you launch new products. Since they are likely to know and trust you, they should be more prepared to listen to the advantages of trading up or replacing. If you don't know what your customers have bought, and when, you may be hurting rather than enhancing the relationships.

Take the situation with cell (mobile) phone providers. Sometimes, just after you have purchased a new phone, they start bombarding you with e-mails and fliers for other new phones. If they were to wait 6 months or a year there would be more innovations, your existing phone would not be quite so shiny and new and you would be more open to change.

It is also a good business strategy to maintain as many existing clients as you can because this will allow you to plan ahead and budget more accurately for the future. The deeper and longer the relationship is, the better are the chances that the client will continue to buy from you, provided the quality of your product or service doesn't change and their business strategy remains the same. This is why it is so important to keep communication open and frequent so that you can anticipate any changes that may occur.

Additionally, a happy customer is the best marketing that anyone can have and a good source of referrals, if you don't neglect to ask for them. Clients' testimonials are the best form of advertising because they gain immediate trust from the potential buyers and they are the best value for money since they are free....

For some businesses Newsletters (printed or digital) and a strong Internet presence in Blogs, Website Forums and Social Media Fan Pages are also a great way to build a community of existing clients and to promote your business to others.

46 Over Dependent on 1 or 2 Customers

A problem that is directly related to excessive focus on new customers is the 'chasing rainbows' syndrome. Some businesses drain too much energy going after the really big deals that would be enough to make the annual budget with just one sale. They also dream of the steady stream of follow-on orders and the credibility that would come with landing a big customer and playing in the big league.

Many business owners feel thrilled about getting a big client and jump head first thinking they have the orders guaranteed for years to come. They forget the small print in the contract that was usually signed on the customers' terms and they don't realize that they will always be competing with large companies that are hungry for those customers and have cost structures that allow them to offer low prices.

The problem is, of course, that the bigger the sale, the bigger the risk (in addition to the fiercer competition). To win a big sale margins have to be reduced, and once you have established that price or discount with the customer you may be held to it in all future transactions with them. High discounts, customized packaging, customized support, extended payment terms etc. represent less revenue and higher costs per sale which may compromise your profitability and cash flow.

Of course we are talking about repeat business here. If your business is in an area where clients make a one off purchase or they won't come back for many years, this situation does not apply.

However, in the case of regular sales, before you go after a big client you need to do your homework and calculate how much of your production capacity or manpower will be used to satisfy the client's needs. If the percentage is significant, this means you won't be able to serve many customers that buy from you at prices that give you higher profit margins.

The next step is to consider the investment needed to increase your production capacity, or provide maintenance services where you may have to recruit more people. If your market is clearly expanding this could be a growth opportunity. Ask your team to make a three year plan and discuss the scenarios with them, including a contingency plan for losing the big client and immediate steps to diversify your client base. Ponder the risk of losing the client at present capacity vs in that scenario. Consider outsourcing to keep the investment effort under control. Very likely you will come to the conclusion that it is too risky to have all your eggs in one basket or that it is a big risk to invest on increased production capacity that you wouldn't use if the big client leaves. Outsourcing may also prove to be the wrong option because of the thin margins you would be working on.

Unless your company has a unique competitive advantage or a contract that guaranties that any big client will stay with you for a long term, it may be wiser to focus on smaller clients in different industries who value your products/services and the personalized attention provided. These clients will most likely be prepared to pay a fairer price for the products or services you offer.

A balanced client mix is an important factor for survival. Not being in the hands of a few clients is important but only selling to one industry or market may also be a risk if there is a specific problem, like a change in technology or legislation.

47 Customer Service

"Customer service is not a department, it's everyone's job."
Anonymous

Poor Customer Service impacts the turnover, bottom line and profit margins in all types of industries and businesses throughout the world.

It can relate to generally unhelpful or impolite staff (usually due to lack of training, knowledge and skill), the quality of the product or service itself, its presentation, price or the bad after sales service (delivery, replacement of faulty item, support). Any issues with the product or service, presentation or price when amplified by unsuitable handling by Customer Services can generate loss of sales because word-of-mouth can spread quickly in the community causing a negative impact on the brand and reputation which can be very hard to shake off.

Successful businesses have Customer Support staff that are aligned with the company's values and mission and are eager to please, leading to a happy customer experience and ultimately more return business.

Ensure that staff who deal with customers on a day to day basis are trained, understand the company's values, know the products/services and have the motivation to go the extra mile to assist customers.

No matter how good your product or service may be, there will always be small problems and, rightly or wrongly, unhappy customers. All complaints should be independently analyzed to ascertain if it was an incident or if it is a recurrent pattern. Although you keep a closer relationship with your main clients, all clients (big or small) need to feel they are treated with respect, get a fair price, efficient delivery, products and services that fit their needs, etc. In the event of something going wrong, all issues should be promptly and efficiently dealt with, because the way any complaint is handled has a great influence on whether the clients will buy from you again or not.

Different products and services require different levels of after sales support. If customers think you have gone the extra mile they are likely to recommend you. If they think that you didn't live up to expectations they will certainly complain to others about the way they were treated. It is up to you to turn your customers into raving fans.

The cost of dealing with customer calls can be quite high. There are a variety of solutions available which can save money, but have some disadvantages:

Automated call systems where the client defines the problem before speaking to a person in the correct department can present some challenges if you are calling from a mobile or old phone. The process is more time consuming and the choices may not be clear.

Call centers in a foreign country with lower labor costs have sometimes unsatisfactory results because people are recruited and trained to work in a call-center with very little knowledge of your products or services and your company's culture. They read from a script and have difficulty in establishing empathy or even effective communication at times.

Online computer systems, the cheapest of all to administer are unfortunately the most dehumanized. A semi-automated solution may work to solve standard issues but is useless when customers have a specific problem.

Some companies make the option of setting up a 'value added calls' system for complaints. This means clients have to pay if they have an issue and want the problem solved, which doesn't seem a fair policy.

The best way to save money in complaints is to ensure you deliver a good product or service and that you have systems in place to minimize the occurrence of issues that may cause a client to complain.

48 Over Focus on Getting Orders

A pipeline of prospects and a constant flow of orders are essential for any business. However, it is important to remember that a sale is not completed until the customer pays.

Salespeople usually think they have done their job when they get the order or the contract signed. It might be so in an ideal world, but too many factors get in the way to allow the process to be as linear and as simple as that. The problems may have its origin in any stage of the sales process, in the delivery or in the product or service itself.

The salesperson may have left some point unclear or may have made promises about specifications, functionality and delivery times which will be difficult to fulfill. If terms and promises are not met, the client may well refuse to pay or if he pays he will be an unsatisfied customer, which will affect the reputation of the business. In this case it is always preferable to take the loss, give a refund or negotiate some sort of compensation, apologize and start over with a clean slate.

Pressure to reach sales goals may lead to accepting orders from customers with bad payment history or bringing in new customers that present a risk due to their financial situation. The company needs to have systems in place to freeze credit to clients that delay payments – which would mean that they can only buy if they pay in cash – or not to grant credit to new customers without doing the due diligence.

Unfortunately, even amongst the clients who pay there are some who bring more problems than revenue. They haggle over prices, quality, delivery times, payment terms etc. A careful evaluation has to be made on the revenue and profits that these clients actually generate and a decision made on whether to refuse to work anymore with them. Alternatively reallocate the account to another salesperson that will have a more assertive position throughout the sales process and reeducate the client into a more reasonable relationship.

In the sales process, as in most situations, quality trumps quantity, so sales, finance, distribution and customer support should work together to assure they maximize the return on sales effort and that the company is up to dealing with the best customers in the market. A well-handled sale will bring more business - repeat orders and referrals.

Due to the nature of some businesses it is standard procedure to have salespeople accountable for the relationship with the customers, not just for the sales. In this case the salesperson will follow the order through to the final delivery, assist on installation or warranty issue and give a subtle hand in collections as well as following up by checking periodically to see that everything is ok. This usually applies to high value sales or key clients but any salesman who monitors the whole process can make his work easier in the future by ensuring the client is really satisfied.

The relationship with potential customers needs to be nurtured sometimes over a long period of time. If an enquiry doesn't result in a sale right away but the potential and interest are there, it could still happen in the future. If salespeople adopt the farmers' approach of sowing seeds instead of the hunters' approach that goes for the kill, the relationship with the potential customer will be nurtured and with follow up may result in a sale or a referral.

49 Inadequate Sales Compensation Plan

One of the biggest management challenges for a growing business is compensating salespeople effectively, since sales incentive plans can have an enormous impact on the bottom line and on the future growth of the company.

The compensation plan must be aligned with the company's mission and values so that it works as a complementary tool to your marketing strategy and motivates the sales force by aligning them with the business goals.

Good compensation plans are designed with the end in mind – the broader growth objectives for the company – then clearly identifying sales-related actions and behaviors that support those objectives and finally tying those to the desired individual performance. This is the best way to ensure that the sales force is motivated and rewarded for behavior and actions that comply with the company's strategy.

So how do you set parameters for performance and measure it?

What is the right balance between base salary and commissions?

What is the standard for your industry?

Some companies pay their sales people with straight salaries; others put their sales people on 100 percent commission. The vast majority of businesses opt for a middle ground. Straight base salaries guarantee income during economic downturns when sales go down and the variable pay incentivizes salespeople to work harder.

All sales compensation plans have to be written down and accessible to the sales force stating clearly what the company is aiming to achieve, the benchmarks and performance measures and the payout formula (straight compensation and commission structure). The compensation plan can't cover all the issues that are going to be raised by the salespeople but it needs to include how any conflict is going to be solved (whether it is by a committee or by the chain of command). This way the rules are clear for everybody.

Most plans are designed to pay for performance but this is a concept that is too vague. Is meeting quarterly sales quotas the right criteria? What if the numbers are met by selling products at a deep discount? Wouldn't it be more important to protect the company's profitability? What about clients' satisfaction? How can you measure that? Should sales to an existing account carry as much weight as signing up a new client?

It all depends on your business objectives. You may want the sales force to focus on a particular product or market, in which case bigger commissions could work as incentive. Commissions should also reward the degree to which a sales person has to work to get a customer to buy a product or service. In some industries, products sell themselves; in other industries customers need to be courted and educated on the benefits of a product or service.

If you have a collaborative sales process involving sales, business development and application engineers, the weight of the commission in the compensation plan should be lower. The same happens in companies that sell big ticket items like aircraft that have a long selling cycle (sometimes years), whereas in a business like selling paper sales and landing new clients happen several times per month, thus the higher variable compensation. The type of business and sales cycle are important factors in the choice of the compensation structure.

While a high risk/reward incentive program may be necessary to attract your ideal sales person, you need to think through the possible consequences namely the impact on a customer's experience. Customers who enter a car dealership or a clothing store can have very different experiences, based on a salesperson's incentive plan (from no action to feeling over pressured).

You may want to hear feedback from the sales manager on how the plan is perceived by the sales force, from a representative of human resources on what the competition is doing, from finance on sales profitability and from sales admin on whether the business is rewarding the right people. However, the company's long-term interests and reputation have to be the most important factors when deciding the compensation plan which includes monitoring the markets to make sure you adjust to any significant changes.

50 Insufficient Motivation

> *'A salesman minus enthusiasm is just a clerk'*
> Harry F Banks (author)

What motivates a sales force?

Having a well-designed and adequate sales compensation plan is important but not enough. You need to have a good understanding of basic human needs and of the methods that can sustain high levels of motivation among the sales staff. If the salespeople are motivated and engaged they will not only have better results but won't think of going and working somewhere else. It is important that you come up with a comprehensive approach to incentive management.

Abraham Maslow's hierarchical understanding of basic or innate human needs, originally set at five levels, can help you to understand your sales team and how to best energize them. The bottom level comprises the physiological needs, the requirements for human survival which need to be covered by the financial compensation.

The next level is the need for safety and security. In a sales context, this can be tied in to the level of trust in the company values and compensation structure. If salespeople don't trust the system or their peers, they waste precious time verifying compensation data, instead of meeting customers and closing deals.

The third level is the need to belong and feel a part of a group. Regular sales team meetings with focus on team work and cooperation amongst them and with other departments to beat the competition will fulfill this need. An annual sales conference, where the team interacts with each other in a forum setting can strengthen the bonds.

The fourth level is the need for achievement and recognition from others. An important motivator for the sales force is the respect from senior management as well as recognition from peers. Positive feedback in sales meetings for great attitude and best practices and a rewards program for high performance with a trip or a place in the 'circle of excellence' are also good motivators.

Finally, at the top of Maslow's hierarchy is self-actualization, or 'growth need', the desire to live up to one's potential. Acquiring new knowledge and skills will enable them to take on ever-greater challenges.

Today's sales environment is very complex. The average selling cycle is getting longer. The number of calls necessary to close a deal has also jumped and conversion rates are going down. Customers have access to multiple markets as well as in-depth information and reviews through the Internet, so their demands and the pressure from competitors continue to rise. To effectively sell solutions, a salesperson needs to keep up with technological advances and have more knowledge across a broader spectrum of products and services.

Some companies predicted this evolution and have been working hard on differentiating their products or services, as well as on designing comprehensive, technology-based tools and training to support their sales force. Technical abilities without a deep understanding of the clients' needs and of the psychology of sales are insufficient and sales skills, as they were defined in the past, have become obsolete.

Nowadays selling is about educating the customer in the process of purchasing and involves working for an organization where the sales process runs as smoothly as possible. Being supported by efficient logistics, admin and customer services can be as motivating for salespeople as compensation incentives because they make it possible for them to reach their full potential.

Main Takeaways:

1.

2.

3.

Improvements to implement:

Action 1.

By:Start Date:Ready by:

Action 2.

By:Start Date:Ready by:

Action 3.

By:Start Date:Ready by:

Organization's Structure

An organization's structure depends entirely on its objectives and on the strategy chosen to achieve them.

In centralized structures, the decision making is concentrated in the top layer of management and tight control is exercised over departments and divisions. In decentralized structures, the decision making power is distributed and departments or divisions have more autonomy.

Small businesses tend to have very centralized structures, since they begin usually with a one or two men team that very often has issues about delegation and letting go of the decision making power.

Finding the ideal structure is part of the growth process of any organization and delegation is a challenge for entrepreneurs. When the owners master the process of leveraging their time and working on the business instead of in the business the company will be in a better position to reach its full potential.

In **www.BusinessGrowthLevers.com/resources** you'll find models for Organization Charts and other tools to support your business.

51 Best Structure for the Business

Most organizations evolved to their present structure, instead of being purposely designed. As a result, the efforts of the individual parts of the organization are only loosely aligned to the business goals, rather than closely aligned.

Organizations don't succeed per se. Success comes from the business owner's capacity to align each individual with the organization's goals, from giving them the autonomy to be creative and, of course, from the individual's performance and contribution.

As a business owner, the sooner you design your organization's structure, the sooner you ensure that the efforts of all the individuals and departments are aligned with the overall strategy and direction. In fact, from the inception you should have an idea of the structure you will need. Draw an organization chart of the functions with no names except your own and anyone who starts the company with you. This can help you in the process of selecting the people who will be working with you as the company grows, to decide what can be outsourced and when is the right moment to start doing an activity in-house.

To fulfill its mission effectively a business needs to operate within a structure that is best suited to its purposes. Typical organization charts are organized by functions and include Production, Marketing and Sales, Finance, Human Resources and Information Systems (if relevant). Each functional area has a Director that will have Managers reporting to them and then assistants or clerks. Large organizations have Presidents and Vice-Presidents but we won't go into that detail because it is not relevant for the scope of this book.

The number of levels of authority depends upon the size of the business and whether the business has a hierarchical or flat structure.

A hierarchical structure has several layers of management, each with a narrow span of control. Instructions feed downwards to the levels below in the chain of command. Feedback comes from the lower levels upwards. This type of structure enables tighter control and offers a clear career path and opportunities for promotion. However, speed of communication can be a problem through all the levels and staff may not feel empowered. Creativity and initiative is limited due to the need to seek approval, which could lead to reduced motivation.

In a flat structure there are few layers of management, so each manager has a wider span of control. This usually means that a manager has responsibility for more people and has little or no time for performing specific tasks. A higher level of people skills is essential to ensure delegated tasks are performed efficiently and most staff will be given greater autonomy in their work. Communication is usually faster, which enables problems to be solved quicker.

If your company is fairly large and has differentiated lines of products, customer segments or geographical locations, a divisional or team structure may be more adequate.

The same applies if your work is organized by project. In this case each division is responsible for a line of products or a project and has its own dedicated resources such as finance, marketing, warehousing, maintenance, etc. This allows differentiation strategies, more flexibility, innovation and a quicker response to environmental changes. However, there can be duplication of resources and low interaction between people working in similar functions.

A matrix structure combines the functional and divisional structures. You can have a functional structure and then assign a manager for each line of products. The downside is that some employees will have two managers - a functional manager and a product manager.

To maximize the company's potential management should take the necessary actions to decrease the disadvantages of the chosen structure and to enhance the positive effects.

52 Flexibility

As a company grows, the organizational structure must change with it.

Organization's Structure

In the early stage entrepreneurs create products or services for which there is a market and the founder is involved in every aspect of the business, making all the decisions usually with no formal structure. As the company grows in size, a more formal structure is needed, the owner can no longer be solely responsible for all decision making and professional managers plan their areas, organize their staff and create written policies and procedures. At this point you may still be outsourcing some areas (like accounting, for example) but the principle is pretty much the same.

As you continue to grow there is the danger that the company's structure becomes too rigid. The different areas won't communicate well and may tend to see themselves as separate teams and blame other areas for any problems that occur. Additionally, lower level employees feel left out and detached from the company as a whole.

With too many layers of management there will be a loss of agility (too much time spent on the decision process or passing on information) and the cost of management will be unduly high. Other consequences could be high bureaucracy, poor teamwork (as each manager protects their turf, their budget and headcount) and lack of accountability because there are too many people involved. If your company gets to this stage, get immediate help!

The company risks losing its identity – it is too big for you to control and the Directors or Managers have got distracted chasing department objectives. They will have lost the company vision, mission and values. The blame game – 'that is Sales problem, not my department' can destroy your business.

The primary team for the Directors is the management team and they should all work together, helping each other fulfill the company's goals. Delegation of duties to lower-level employees, focusing on motivating people followed up by coaching will be the solution that will allow senior executives to devote more of their time to long term management issues and get the company back on track.

A consultant will have a more objective and detached view of inefficiencies or weaknesses in an organization but you are the one who knows the business, the logic and the reasons why things are organized the way they are. You may find consultants who try to change the structure to either one they have installed before in another company, or to the 'flavor of the month'. That is definitely not what you need!

The best use of a consultant or business coach is to help you come up with the solution for your business based on your knowledge of it and your vision. This way you will be able to understand the changes, communicate them to your staff and be in control of the situation.

What is your strategy?

How many products do you have?

What type of technology are you using?

How big is your company/organization?

How is it spread geographically?

The objective of a structure is to organize the staff in a way that allows you to coordinate activities by clearly identifying which individuals are responsible for which tasks in order to meet the company's goals. It is very important to select the structure that best serves your business at the present moment and into the future. A structure that has evolved may creak and groan but you have to repair it with care. If you try to fit a turbo charger on an old car you may need to put wider tires, better breaks and a new drive shaft to handle the extra power.

Any alterations to the structure or systems must be thoroughly planned and test run, or run in parallel, if possible. Additionally they must produce objective and measurable results when compared to other similar businesses or to the previous situation of your business.

53 Policies and Procedures

When an organization starts with a few staff, it may seem unnecessary and a waste of time to develop formal procedures, worry about who should be doing what or how information should be passed on and stored. There is a tendency to grow procedures organically over time. However, as an organization grows the absence of a Policies and Procedures Manual can lead to fundamental inefficiencies, especially duplicated work.

Members of staff who have been with the company for some time have routines - the way their tasks have always been done. However, a procedure that made sense in the past may no longer add value due to changes, but they keep on doing it just the same because no one has taken the time to evaluate its use and effectiveness.

The investment in establishing formal procedures improves efficiency and minimizes conflicts about how things should be done. If you want your company to carry out its mission successfully, you must develop a functioning internal structure and have systems that allow the staff to perform their work effectively thus being more efficient and credible.

Organizing a business is generally assumed to include having systems and procedures that give logical flows of tasks, usually in a linear and chronological order. These systems and procedures can contemplate recurring tasks or exceptional occurrences, like a fire. The point is to ensure 'best practices' are followed, that you don't have to make every decision as guesswork is eliminated and errors reduced.

The methodology for establishing procedures includes meeting with the members of the staff involved and identifying what can be systematized. The next step is to break it down into components and analyze each one, identifying flaws, bottlenecks, limiting factors and inefficiencies to create solutions and opportunities for improvement. The proposed new procedures should be written down step by step in detail, documented and reviewed.

Ensure that all people who will be impacted by the system or procedure fully understand it and buy into it. Train them so that the new procedure becomes ingrained, automatic and routine. Staff should be actively encouraged to suggest improvements in processes, but not authorized to make any unapproved changes.

Where you have more than one location it might be beneficial to experiment with new procedures in just one of them before implementing it across the whole organization.

The systems and internal procedures developed should be compiled in the form of a Manual. Staff can then easily refer to it when needed and new people can quickly orient themselves by this document. The process of preparing and organizing the Manual will pinpoint areas where no procedures exist, but need to be designed. It will also improve already existing procedures, since while writing them down people often see ways to make them more effective.

The Manual will be more useful if it includes descriptive visual depictions to accompany procedural text like process maps and charts to explain the flow. Once these structures and systems are in place they will be helpful if a dispute arises. Instead of arguing, both sides can consult the record that was commonly agreed and use it as a guide.

A clear set of policies and procedures for every area across the business will allow the company to conduct business in a consistent manner. If you open an office or branch in another location or decide to open a new business with similar characteristics you can replicate the system.

Think about it. Would ensuring that everyone is following the same procedures improve company operations?

Do staff know everything they need to about customer requirements?

Is it important to you that everyone at all levels of the company be able to describe the company goals and objectives when asked?

Do you think your employees feel involved and committed to continuous improvement?

This is the power of a clearly written Manual.

54 Outsourcing Enough

Outsourcing is a strategy that organizations have been increasingly using to avoid heavy structures and to remain as flexible as possible.

The use of specialized and efficient service providers to perform activities traditionally handled by internal staff can improve company focus, reduce and control operating costs, reduce risk and gain access to better trained professionals.

In rapid growth periods – either during the first couple of years or when the company is expanding - back-office operations need to be reinforced.

It is advisable to keep the focus on the core business and use outsourcing until you are sure that the growth is permanent and then evaluate if it is more efficient to remain as you are or allocate the time and money to restructure your internal resources.

If your company is small, you will have access to better professionals at lower cost because you will only be using part of their time while being able to contact them when required (unlike a part-time employee).

You may also consider outsourcing some simple operations to reduce the need for office space if rent is a significant cost and make use of lower labor costs in other locations.

By outsourcing to a reputable company you won't have to worry about absenteeism or poor management because you transfer that responsibility to the service provider. This can also be useful with low skilled work where the turnover is high – the provider is responsible for recruiting the staff to make sure someone always turns up. The same applies for operations that have seasonal or cyclical demands.

If you start working with a big client and are not sure how things will turn out, it would be wise to outsource for a period matching the initial contract length until you can assess if you are going to keep the client.

Another situation would be if you undertake a project that requires skills your staff don't have. Outsourcing would be a solution since it can save time and reduce the risk of not recruiting the right people.

Common areas for outsourcing are:

Secretarial Work - typing, making appointments and travel bookings either on-site or in another location also known as virtual assistants.

Accounting, Financial and Tax Services - billing, payroll processing, preparing financial statements and tax forms, etc.

Human Resources - recruitment, employee benefits admin. etc.

Customer Support - routine customer support calls can be answered by a call center located anywhere (see also **47.**).

Marketing - advertising campaigns, telemarketing and public relations.

Distribution - usually to carriers like UPS or FedEx.

Information Technologies (IT) – the use of data centers saves the investment in equipment, software, maintenance and replacement due to technological evolution.

In these areas, the significant amount of demand has resulted in the existence of a wide variety of providers.

Outsourcing should be viewed as a way to increase the quality of your services and not just a way to cut costs. Ongoing management of the relationship is paramount to keep quality standards high. Senior management must stay involved and meet at appropriate intervals to discuss the areas for improvement and keep the outsourcing relationship a fruitful one. Providers usually try to win the initial contract by offering better or more comprehensive services at lower prices than they can really provide. It is up to you to hold them to their promises or change provider before it compromises the reputation of your business.

55 Outsourcing Too Much

The outsourcing craze has resulted from the need that companies have to stay flexible. Nobody knows what tomorrow will bring so the whole process of recruiting, training, supervising, coaching and motivating has scared a lot of entrepreneurs who have opted to have task performance solved with the same ease as buying a car.

However, the perception that outsourcing companies will do it better because they specialize is only partly true. Although they should have higher technical ability and more experience, their motivation is to reduce their own costs in order to maximize their profits.

Another common mistake is thinking that an outsourcing will be cheaper. This can be true if you are small and only need part time or temporary services, but for full time assignments it is obvious that it will be more expensive, since they have to make a profit.

Your cost/benefit analysis may have additional factors to consider (like office costs) but it must remain objective to this point.

Finally, the idea that outside professionals will be more productive than internal staff is also a myth. It can be, to start with, especially if there is a trial period… There are no miracles! If an outsourcing company claims that they handle a lot more calls in the same period, for example, it usually just means they are not putting the same quality and attention into answering whoever they are dealing with.

Make sure the contract protects your company and invest time in negotiating every detail. Remember that although outsourcing is undoubtedly a very useful resource and the best option in a number of situations, you will always be dealing with independent contractors, so you have little or no control over their business.

Whether you sign a contract to have another company perform the function of an entire department or just a single task, you are handing over management and control to them. The contract may be designed to protect you, but the fact remains that another company will control the process. This means that the vendor selection needs to be very thorough, since you have to make sure that your company's mission, values and culture are not jeopardized.

You have got to do your due diligence on the standards and quality of the service delivered by your future 'partners' such as how long they have been operating in the market and who the other clients they serve are. Make sure that they are providing real value, there are no hidden costs and that confidentiality and quality are being assured.

Senior management must articulate the goals and objectives of the outsourcing initiative and communicate how the process will benefit the organization. Then, if outsourcing is the best option, the knowledge that your own staff has about the function and how it relates to your business needs to be seamlessly integrated.

It is important to keep the control as much as possible within your company. Hence you reduce the risk of any drop in quality, data security and privacy compliance and have the ability to bring the process back in-house. Bear in mind that once you are locked-in with outsourcing it can be difficult to go back to in-house quickly.

Main Takeaways:

1.

2.

3.

Improvements to implement:

Action 1.

By: Start Date: Ready by:

Action 2

By: Start Date: Ready by:

Action 3.

By: Start Date: Ready by:

Organization's Culture

The Organization's Culture includes the attitudes, values, beliefs and behaviors that are expressed in the way an organization positions itself in the market, the way it treats the employees, customers and the community, as well as the actual environment.

These are often unwritten rules that have evolved over time and hence each individual will have a unique perspective depending on where they are in the organization, how they have been treated in the past and how they expect to be treated in the future.

In **www.BusinessGrowthLevers.com/resources** you will find some tips and tools to assist you with your Organization's Culture.

56 Repairing a Damaged Culture

Cultures develop in organizations influenced primarily by its leaders, the mission and values and then as a result of adaptation to the market and social environment along with internal dynamics.

The culture incorporates the company's history and the stories that result from the way it grows, the way it is organized and generates profit - its structure, systems and staff interactions internally and with clients, suppliers and stakeholders in general.

A strong culture provides a better sense of direction for the staff keeping them more motivated and productive thus making the organization more efficient in achieving its goals. On the other hand, in a weak culture there is little alignment between the staff and the organization's values which increases the need for control and can limit creativity and job satisfaction.

Culture, like reputation, develops gradually and is very hard to change for the better in the short term. However, serious damage can be done to the culture in an instant with what might seem a small negative incident if left to grow out of proportion or if it goes against the organizations' values. Take employee lay-offs rumors, for example. If not handled with care, these result in stress, fear, bad feelings and loss of productivity and creativity that will impact the business.

Hierarchy and titles in particular can have a large influence on culture. They may be essential in situations where rules and procedures are critical, such as health care, where decision making is based on knowledge and experience. Where ideas, innovation and problem solving are necessary, for example in an advertising agency, a less formal culture is more beneficial.

'Actions speak louder than words' is a proverb, or figure of speech that particularly applies in relation to culture. If you preach the virtues of employee safety but then don't buy appropriate safety equipment or flaunt the safety rules yourself, people will know this is not an important issue for you. Consequently employee safety will not get the attention that it deserves.

Attracting the right staff depends just as much on the remuneration package as it does on the company culture.

Walking into the premises for the first time - the environment, including things like the furniture style, color of the walls and flooring, paintings and pictures, noise level etc. may only have an effect at the subconscious level but is very important both for clients and future employees. Although candidates may not be aware of details like the carpet color or the furniture, these things play an important part in how they feel about the business and whether they take the job or not.

Sub-cultures can often exist in departments where the department head allows or encourages things to differ from the accepted norms for the rest of the company. The effect can be very beneficial in some cases like a Research and Development department where everything is a bit crazy, but amazing things come out of it.

In contrast, a department where rules are ignored may cause friction with other departments and undermine the whole company's culture. Sub-cultures need to be aligned with the basic values and beliefs and discouraged early if they risk contaminating the overall environment.

Although culture isn't easy to define or pin down to a few sentences, all great companies have a discernible strong culture that works like an invisible bond between all those that work for it.

57 Making it about 'Us'

> *"Alone we can do so little; together we can do so much"*
> Helen Keller

We live in a competitive society where being first has an overwhelming importance. Even in team sports focus is mainly on the stars of the team. To really inspire your team and get everyone working for the good of the company the whole culture must revolve around the concept of 'our' company. Everyone needs to have a sense of ownership and belonging.

This transition has to start with you, as owner (or CEO) in the way you talk and behave. When you are talking about your business you need to stop using 'I' and 'my' and change them to 'we', 'us' and 'our'.

Intelligent leaders understand the need to foster a culture of teamwork and team spirit. From the moment you think of bringing someone to work in your organization share the company's values and mission with them and if you feel they don't share the values or are not team players don't bring them on board.

Encourage cooperative efforts at all levels across the company, establish clear individual and team expectations and hold them accountable for results.

It is important to recognize individual performance and value creativity and suggestions for improvement without fear of judgment or finger pointing. Thank them in the name of the team. This way the organization always comes first but there is still respect shown for those who have gone beyond what is normally expected.

A participatory workplace will be more stimulating and common business objectives will be achieved quicker and more efficiently. Mutual trust and teamwork will make the company's culture stronger. Consensus will be built with the staff really feeling their input was considered and there is no 'boss and workers' situation.

As the company grows and becomes more successful you need to ensure the attention moves away from yourself, and what you are doing, and more to the company and 'the team'. To have your name and photograph mentioned in a newspaper or magazine does a lot for the ego, but it could do much more for the team if the emphasis was clearly on them.

In most organizations there is a lot of internal competition, for example, to be the best performing salesman or collectively the best performing team. While this competition is usually healthy beware if cheating creeps in as the company will suffer. Rules and metrics should be crystal clear and any less ethical behavior severely punished. How does a salesman react when he hears of a possible lead outside his area? Does he pass it on to his colleague, or does he ignore it because he will see no personal benefit? If you have managed to create a culture of true cooperation your staff will always behave in the best interest of the organization, which will ultimately be their own best interest too.

Internal competition may bring short term gains. External competition against another company can bring medium term gains. Aiming to be the best, for the benefit of society as a whole, can be much more powerful and longer lasting.

58 Increase Quality

"Be a yardstick of quality.
Some people aren't used to an environment where excellence is expected."
Steve Jobs

Company culture is, in a way, the driving force to its overall success and the attitude towards quality is very much a part of the equation. The best and most successful companies understand the need to create a culture where a stimulating internal environment and the creation of delighted customers go together. For that there has to be a pursuit for continuous improvement.

Quality Circles originated in Japan in the early 60's. Groups of employees, usually with a supervisor, looked at ways to improve products and processes. Changes in attitude with development of both individual and team spirit not only improve products and processes but have a positive influence on motivation and the organizational culture. This evolved into TQM (Total Quality Management) and 6 Sigma (a methodology for reducing defects by minimizing variations in processes) along with the Quality certification for organizations.

Careful evaluation is needed to determine the cost of improving quality including how much this will reduce other costs, influence sales and customer satisfaction. This is now a specialized area and professional help should be sought to reach the higher levels.

Poor quality will always impact the future of the company. This could be via costs for repair or substitution of returned goods, additional maintenance costs or low customer satisfaction, which results in a loss of future business. Dealing with customer complaints costs time and money and if poorly handled will result in an ex-customer who will willingly tell everyone what a bad business you run.

Improving quality has a price, which is usually exponential. To start with, the cost of improving is often small, for example training staff to take more care and motivate them to perform better. The more systems and quality controls you implement, the more expensive it becomes to reach higher levels of quality. It may require new machines for production that use new technology to manufacture with higher precision or more extensive testing.

Although this is a reality it is also true that Quality is a way of 'being' in business. Take the time to interact with your staff, your Clients and your Suppliers and ask the right questions. Understand what are your product or service strengths and areas for improvement as well as your competitors'. You can use then optimize what you offer to your clients and exceed their expectations. Do not miss an opportunity to ask for feedback and be consistent and honest in all your interactions with others (internally and externally).

Quality does not relate only to the products and services that go out to customers. It involves all other aspects of the business. For example, internal communications with other departments have to be clear and timely. Informing the Logistics department late in the day that a large shipment is about to arrive could cause bad feeling as well as disruption because of the loading dock and warehouse not being prepared.

Quality is doing the right thing at the right time in the best possible way for the long term good. Before making any major investment to improve 'quality' you have to be sure of what your clients or prospects value and what will be the end result of such investment. This means your approach should be more results oriented than feature oriented.

It is up to each business owner and his team to decide what are the necessary steps to assure that growth, profitability, customer satisfaction and a healthy work environment are best achieved.

59 Productive Meetings

> *"Meetings are indispensable when you don't want to do anything."*
> *John Kenneth Galbraith (Canadian Economist)*

Meetings, and the way they are conducted, form a part of the culture and its' evolution. You have to have meetings to inform, be informed and interact. It is important to be face to face with others so that you can see the body language, not just hear their voice as you would over the phone or merely see the words in an e-mail. Some things have to be done in a group setting where people may have different views and ideas that need to be discussed. An e-mail is often too impersonal and can take too long when issues need a back and forth to be resolved.

Meetings, however, can be an enormous waste of time if unnecessary and not well run. They should always have a specific objective like information sharing, motivating, brain storming or decision making and follow up action. When you have periodic meetings the main objective may be forgotten over time, focus lost and office politics take over. A clear agenda sent by e-mail a suitable time before can be used to get people on track, especially if information needs to be prepared.

If key people can't attend and their input is important, don't hold the meeting just because it was scheduled for that time. Cancel or postpone it. If their input is not so important, just make sure they get a copy of the minutes. Similarly, don't invite people just so they don't feel left out. Good leadership and management include not wasting other people's time but still keeping them informed and motivated.

Although it can be difficult to set a time for each point on the agenda the start and finish should be clear and kept to as much as possible.

The more interaction and creativity is required the less predictable will be the time needed. Put the most important items first and the less important at the end, so that if the meeting is running late less time is spent on lesser items or they are postponed. If you finish early then it is unlikely that anyone will object unless they had a point on the agenda that was not properly dealt with.

Don't tolerate interruptions unless they are critical. Interruptions break the flow of the meeting which affects your schedule as well as everyone else's. Keep the meeting on track without letting anyone monopolize it or get away from the agenda unless it is a major issue.

Minutes should be taken but don't waste time reading minutes of prior meetings. These should have been sent out after the last meeting and read and approved by those who were present. Bring a copy as they may need to be referred to if there were decisions or action items from the last meeting that impact the running of the current one.

If there are no action steps that come out of a meeting, why was it held in the first place? If it was just to inform those who were present of something, then an e-mail might have been more efficient. You, or the leader of the meeting, have to ensure that people are held responsible and there is follow up on the action items and deliverables, otherwise the meeting, or part of it, will have been a waste of time. Whoever controls the agenda has the power to ensure that all important issues are discussed and followed up by action steps and tangible results.

If run properly meetings will be productive instead of like James T. Kirk says *"A meeting is an event where minutes are taken and hours wasted".*

60 Resistance to Change

"Nothing endures but change."
Heraclitus (540 BC - 480 BC)

We have already looked at how you personally deal with change, so now we are going to examine how the organization relates to it. An organization's ability to deal with change can be improved with the right mindset and the right culture.

Besides the natural resistance to change that all human beings share, employees often fear change because they worry about the survival of their job or their ability to adapt to whatever is new. However, if an organization and its members are not prepared to continuously change and improve, they may compromise the survival of the business.

There are two levels of organizational change – evolutionary change and revolutionary change.

Evolutionary is by definition incremental and linked to continuous improvement in the organization. Small changes, tweaks to systems and procedures or even the implementation of a new software package are part of the natural evolution people accept without major problems, although in many cases they would prefer to stick to what is known and not to have to go through the trouble of learning new things.

Occasionally a revolutionary change occurs – major technological progress may result in your product or production process becoming obsolete, cheaper products from Asia may flood the market, legislation may change or mergers and acquisitions impact your business's environment. A major reorganization or system redesign will need to be made which will require a whole new vision, strategy and even repurposing of the organization.

Change will have to be driven by a project team of staff from various departments, to ensure all cross functional issues are addressed. The key skills managers must have to lead a revolutionary change are communication, team-building and constructive two way feed-back.

Leaders who see themselves as 'the savior' without which the organization could not survive will compromise the process because they will not allow the employees and lower-level managers to get involved in assessing the problems and identifying solutions. Staff will create resistance to the implementation and course correcting of the actions needed. Individuals are always more willing to support and go the extra mile for what they have helped to create.

A good leader must remain aware that change will always cause fear and stress. One of the problems with the human brain is emotions have a stronger influence than logic and fear and stress may cause procrastination. On the other hand, emotions change frequently so a support system of logic is needed to ensure that change happens.

The emotion of a BHAG (Big Hairy Audacious Goal) also has to have small logical steps to get there. The emotion of peer pressure works best with the logic of the peer support. A winning mindset (how good this is going to be when done) accomplishes more coupled with examples that point the way. If the culture is one where goals are normally set with deadlines, individuals are held accountable and there is a positive supportive atmosphere, there is a better chance of change being made successfully.

Change will be more successful if planned proactively instead of occurring as a reaction to events outside your control. However, avoid change for its' own sake or because others did it. Becoming obsessed with change can result in failure to gain the benefits of the last implementation. The consequence of too much change will be lack of commitment for the 'flavor of the month'.

Main Takeaways:

1.

2.

3.

Improvements to implement:

Action 1.

By: Start Date: Ready by:

Action 2.

By: Start Date: Ready by:

Action 3.

By: Start Date: Ready by:

Human Capital

"Find a job you enjoy and you'll never work another day in your life."
Confucius

Human Resources are the people who work in a business.

This concept has evolved to Human Capital to reflect the added value people bring into the organization. Whatever you call them, the people have come to be the differentiator for organizations and the actual basis for their competitive advantage.

Today's big challenges are to align individual career goals with those of the business and to keep consistency within the organization.

In **www.BusinessGrowthLevers.com/resources** you will find some tools to support you in dealing with what can be your biggest resource.

61 Recruiting the Right People

"The key is: Listen closely. Get in the candidate's skin. Why a person left a job or jobs tells you more about them than almost any other piece of data."
Jack Welch (Chairman and CEO of General Electric)

Any company who wants to succeed needs to have the proper expertise in all the key areas.

For that, the right people have to be recruited, integrated into the development process and managed so that everyone forms a team focused on the achievement of the development goals.

Before you begin recruiting you need to determine which areas require the addition of personnel and establish priorities. You need to produce a job description with the tasks that the position entails, the objectives of the function, the performance criteria, and decide which characteristics (skills and personality) the ideal candidate must possess.

Getting the right person for the job is not easy. Every organization wants to attract, motivate and retain the most qualified employees that match the requirements of the job openings. Identify and prioritize the key requirements needed for the position and the special qualifications, traits, characteristics and experience you are seeking in the candidate. Put these in writing because they will be the guide for the interview and for the ad that you may place in the newspaper, post in specialized sites and in your company's website (it adds credibility to know that your company is growing). An alternative is to look internally or ask for your staff to refer a friend.

Job descriptions should tell the candidate exactly what you want and expect from the person selected. A job description is unique and should be adapted before using it again for the same function. If you know your industry you should know the market salary rate for the job. If you don't, ask an expert or research other job adverts.

If you are looking for a key position seek help from professional recruiters. Don't overestimate your interviewing skills. Make sure the person who screens the candidates' applications is qualified to do it. This is a very important task and will save wasted interviews. Make sure all candidates are interviewed at least twice and by two different people. Interviewers should fill out some form that makes it easy to select the candidates for the second interview and that ensures that all aspects are covered (technical, motivational, personnel, plus compensation expectations).

Consider very carefully if the candidate's expectations fit your existing salary levels. Getting the experienced or qualified person that you really need is important but you should avoid having to increase salaries for existing staff or risk discontent over opening an exception.

Once you've identified the right person in terms of skills and experience, make sure they have the right attitude and values. The higher the position the more important this is, since the impact on the future of the company will be greater. Attitude trumps skills and experience. If the person has left the prior job soon after being trained it may show a lack of commitment and loyalty. Another type to avoid is the 'victim' that always blames others.

If you are confident you have the right person, proceed with an offer letter and also provide the job description and the Company Non-Compete or Confidentiality Agreement.

Schedule a starting date that will ensure that the integration runs smoothly – it is imperative that the new employee gets quality time with his colleagues and the people he will be reporting to.

62 Lack of Orientation (Onboarding)

After investing time and money to get the right person you want them to fit in and be productive as quickly as possible. A good onboarding process is key to their success and yours although it is also about how they fit with their colleagues.

The sooner the new employees learn what is expected of them and what to expect from others the less mistakes they will make. If the orientation is not planned, the employee won't feel welcome, will experience anxiety, will feel lost and less enthusiastic. Even for staff with previous working experience the first day in a new job they don't know what to do, who anyone is or how things work.

Many companies have employees' handbooks. The general purpose of the handbook is to provide a guide with policies, procedures, benefits and standards of conduct for the company. Usually it also includes a brief history, the organization chart, the vision, mission, values and goals and a welcome message from the CEO. Even for small businesses, a basic handbook is important because it is the first contact with the company's culture. It shows personalized concern and makes the new employee feel part of an organized community.

Induction needs to be adjusted to the experience of the employee, the complexity of the job and particularities of the organization. Prepare for the employee's first day by having everything ready for his or her arrival - the desk, computer, software programs, mail access and an email account. The office, cubicle or working area should look pleasant and clean. Small details like having the necessary cupboard space and stationary available shouldn't be neglected.

Give the person time to settle down and get familiar with the surroundings. Make sure the new employee gets introduced to everyone and organize brief meetings with the person he or she reports to and the key co-workers. Time spent taking care of paperwork with human resources should be kept to a minimum by having a set organized procedure for newcomers.

If appropriate, assign a mentor to the person and make sure there is a work plan and plenty of support during the first few weeks. Induction can be overwhelming, especially if there is a lot of detail. While it is important to explain how the work fits in the overall scheme of the business there is no need to explain all of it on the first day.

Make sure the new employee has lunch with the co-workers. The impressions the new employee forms during the first few days will have an enormous impact on his attitude and you want to make it positive, affirming, and exciting. On-boarding done right improves new employee productivity, accelerates results and talent retention.

One of the main reasons people change jobs (by their own initiative) is because they never feel part of the organization they have joined. Orientation shows that the organization values them and helps provide the tools necessary for succeeding in the job.

63 Improving Training and Development

More and more business owners realize that developing the skills and knowledge of their workforce through a custom designed Training Programs is a business imperative that can enhance productivity and give them a competitive edge in recruiting and retaining high quality employees. Rapid change requires a skilled, knowledgeable workforce with employees who are adaptive, flexible, and focused on the future. Enhancing employee skills can increase individual and organizational performance besides helping to achieve business results and promoting a stimulating work environment.

Training and Development provides an opportunity to interact with other members of staff in a different setting, strengthening the sense of team work, team spirit and inter-team collaboration. It also helps to improve the organization's culture and effectiveness. Training and Development builds the positive perception and feeling that the organization cares about quality and invests in the employees, creating a win-win situation.

Management (with or without help from outside consultants) should perform needs assessments of the types of training required, determine the best means of delivering it and create the content, attaching standards or measures to each element to be able to evaluate its efficiency.

Some factors involved in determining to what extent training is needed include the complexity of the work environment and the rapid pace of organizational and technological change. The organization's mission and vision are also determinant factors. To design a meaningful and effective training experience you must be aware of people's learning styles and personality types and structure it so that it is fun! Evaluate the results and always consider innovative methods like mentoring and coaching as a complement to consolidate what is learnt in formal training environment.

Advances in learning theory have provided insights into how people learn and how training can be organized most effectively. Training can be provided in a classroom by external or in-house trainers with manuals and appropriate material, or it can be 'on-the-job' supervised by a peer or mentor. Another option if you want to give more freedom to the 'student' is to provide computer-assisted training in a password protected platform where all the materials – audio, videos, self-paced instructional guides and evaluation tests – can be found.

Employee development and training programs can have the objective of just providing the professional and technical skills needed or be much more comprehensive and aim at developing the whole individual and interpersonal skills, thus ensuring his or her career development in the organization. Employees with upgraded skills, working to their full potential and equipped to deal with the changing demands of the workplace will have higher career satisfaction, productivity and motivation.

It is important to set up leadership or executive grooming programs for current executives and employees who aspire to move up in the organization. Training develops people, improves performance, quality, customer satisfaction, productivity, morale, management succession, business development and profitability. All these factors should be taken into consideration when evaluating the effectiveness of the training because the cost benefit analysis may fall short if all aspects are not taken into consideration.

A comprehensive training will also have a more medium/long term impact in the employees' attitude which will help the organization achieve better results and meet its strategic goals.

64 Improving Communication

> *"The single biggest problem in communication is the illusion that it has taken place."*
> George Bernard Shaw (*playwright, co-founder of the London School of Economics*)

Effective communication matters because business organizations are made up of people.

Any type of communication – verbal or written, internal or external – is the key to the development of the culture and performance of the organization since it is the main process of transmitting information, ideas, thoughts, opinions and plans, and creating the sense of community that makes the organization thrive.

The 21st century workplace is characterized by flatter organizations where managers have to interact with many people, some over whom they have no formal control. This means that communication is the key to building trust, foster understanding, empower and motivate others.

The workforce is growing more diverse in age, ethnic heritage, physical abilities and sexual orientation which is an advantage in terms of experiences, perspectives, talents and creativity. However, this puts strain on the effectiveness of the communication to get the productive collaboration the organization needs to maximize its potential.

Specialized business knowledge is important, but it is not enough to guarantee success. Communication skills are vital at all levels, and every organization must make sure that they are moving towards more concise, clear, complete and considerate forms of communication. There needs to be upwards communication (staff to managers), downwards communication (managers to staff) and communication amongst peers.

Management needs to make sure that the information and instructions passed on to their staff are clear. This involves not just precision in the wording but also transparency as to the expected results. Positive and constructive feedback is also a very important part of communication since it lets the employees know how well they have performed and what they can do to improve.

In oral communication there is much more than the words you use. It is also about how you say it – your body language, eye contact, posture, the tone of voice, pitch and speed at which you are talking. It is important to keep consistency between your body language, the way you sound and the words that come out of your mouth to make communication clear and not jeopardize trust.

In written communication words are all you have, so your message should be clear, purposeful and concise with the correct words to avoid any misinterpretation of your message.

Story telling is a technique that is broadening its scope and is frequently applied in organizations to make communication more effective. The idea behind it is that you need to attach emotion to the message if you want it to be remembered and better understood.

All important instructions should be put in writing and minutes of relevant meetings kept after being reviewed and approved by the participants.

With effective communication you can maintain good human relations in the organization and, by encouraging ideas or suggestions from employees and implementing them whenever possible, you can keep them engaged and improve the organization's results.

A company Newsletter, for instance, is an excellent way of complementing the formal everyday business related communication that occurs within an organization. Introducing a new staff member, sharing wins like a new contract that has been signed or an interview given to the press by the owner will strengthen the employee's ties to your organization and increase motivation and team spirit.

65 No Career Planning

Financial instability, intensifying competition, increasing customer expectations and declining resources have kept many companies too busy to worry about career management in their organizations. After all, when you are fighting for survival, everything else seems like unimportant details. However, this attitude may cost the organization in terms of quality, performance and morale because it risks losing the best people or not being able to attract the right talent.

Organizational effectiveness depends on the management's ability to provide tools and resources to their staff to ensure maximum person-job match, skills acquisition and continual improvement for their own career growth and development including alignment between personal goals and those of the organization.

Career Management is a three-way partnership between employees, management and the organization. Employees take ownership of their professional development, management facilitates the process and the organization provides support.

If the company has a good career planning system, management and HR will be aware of the interests, skills and aspirations of candidates and employees to determine their values, passions, strengths and goals and they will know the existing and future opportunities for growth within the organization. This will facilitate the enrolment of the top achievers and the retention of the top performers, motivating them to fully use their potential, talents and capabilities in the best possible ways. A structured, clear career plan also shows that the organization believes in providing fairness and equal opportunities to all employees.

A well-structured and integrated career planning system needs to include a Competency Model which defines for each job position the required technical and behavioral competencies against which the employee can be evaluated. The competency gaps can be addressed and rectified with formal or on-the-job training, coaching, mentoring, etc.

The next step is to have an evaluation process for the respective competences which identifies the differences between the current employee's profile and the ideal version. The results help employees to gain a clear perspective of where they need to improve. This evaluation process must be transparent, objective and measurable so that it can be fair. Periodic evaluation helps determining the progression of the employee and the corrective steps to take.

A well designed and well implemented performance appraisal system will assess the employees both on their existing jobs and on their potential for higher level jobs. The strengths and weaknesses demonstrated will allow the organization to evaluate which (if any) are the possible options for career progression in the organization. Job rotation, job enrichment and job transfers are possible ways to prepare the employees to take on other responsibilities.

In the case of failure to achieve reasonable performance after adequate time, there is a mismatch between the person and the job. If progress can be made and both parties are willing to invest the time and effort, additional development of their competencies should be provided. If not, the working relationship should be terminated.

Career Management changes the focus from evaluating job performance based solely on the organization's needs to aligning this process with the employees' goals and a rewarding career. By matching the employees' evolving interests and competencies with opportunities in the organization the company will enjoy high levels of employee engagement and performance, because people are doing work at which they excel and that they enjoy.

In an increasingly competitive labor market, the quality of the employees you attract and retain, and the steps you take to develop them, will determine the future success and sustainability of your organization.

66 Improving Performance

Any organization expects good or excellent performance from their employees, which means they are achieving their goals in an effective and efficient manner and that those goals are aligned with the overall goals of the organization.

To be able to evaluate performance, any evaluator needs to know the function's objectives and the organization's goals to assess at the same time that the alignment exists. Sometimes there are technological or market changes that alter the importance or validity of some factors so it is important that the evaluation criteria are kept up to date.

Employees can be very busy without being high-performing if their roles are not directly contributing toward achieving the overall goals of the organization. Each person should know exactly what is expected from them and be able to recognize success when they reach it, gaining a strong sense of fulfillment for achieving the goals.

Performance is a function of both ability and motivation. Motivation has to come from within, it is not something you learn on a training course and the triggers are different for each person. The same event can motivate one employee and destroy another one's motivation.

If the problem is motivation, most organizations don't have the time or resources to work through each employee's issues. Unless it is something obvious like a personality clash with the hierarchy that can be solved with coaching at both levels, the employee must go rather than finding a temporary fix that will only postpone the inevitable.

If the problem is ability and training has not bridged the gap, asses if the work environment is providing the necessary resources and consider assigning the person to another job. If poor performance only shows in a small percentage of the responsibilities inherent to the function, evaluate whether it would be beneficial for the organization to remove that part of the work and assign it to somebody else.

Poor performers can compromise goal achievement resulting in less sales, revenue and profitability. Companies who tolerate poor performance may see their high performers leave because they are not happy working in such an environment, so action must be taken fast.

If the start time is important and an employee has been consistently late, specify the frequency or amount of time. Be specific and avoid exaggerated or judgmental statements like "You are totally unreliable". Also make sure he or she understands that coming in late is not acceptable and hurts the organization.

Make it a priority to give immediate focused feedback to all employees. Balanced feedback provides information on what is being done well as well as what could be improved. Positive feedback builds confidence and reinforces behaviors you want to see more of. Negative feedback should be given factually and with suggestions for improvement. Make sure all staff members in your organization that have people reporting to them give appropriate and timely feedback.

It is important to be aware that each person may have a differently reaction when receiving feedback (even under identical circumstances). Positive feedback provides validation, but if exaggerated may convey an overrated opinion of the person's performance. Negative feedback can be taken personally and result in a defensive behavior, but in other cases it can be appreciated because it points out the areas that need to be worked on and gives an opportunity for improvement.

If an employee consistently underperforms and takes negative feedback defensively, make sure he has been given clear indication of what is expected of him. Check that his onboarding was done properly and that he is aware of the written personnel policies. Give him fair warnings and memos describing the degrading performance over time despite the organization's support and assistance. Consult other managers and if you decide to fire the employee, do so promptly. Be quick to write a letter of termination. Hire slow, fire fast as they say.

67 Performance Reviews

Performance reviews are probably the interactions that cause the most fear, aggravation and resentment both on the boss or manager's side and on the direct report's side. Managers dislike them because they usually deal in 'intangibles', they don't always have the documented examples to back up a point and no one likes giving bad news. Employees see it as a threat when communication with the hierarchy is insufficient and they don't receive adequate and frequent feedback on their performance.

Some managers have 10 minute performance reviews with their people, usually in the last week before they are due, and keep it vague and superficial. Other times they only talk about recent events and opinions from others which shows not much thought or preparation was given to the review. Even worse are the managers that use the previous year's performance review, making minimal changes. The message sent is that they are too busy to let staff know how to improve their performance.

There are also managers who say they don't need to do a formal review because their people know they can come to them to talk about anything at any time. Even when this is true, most employees won't go to their bosses to talk about their difficulties in performing their duties.

If induction was done properly the employees have job descriptions and goals set in writing with clear notes on what is expected of them and how their performance is going to be measured and evaluated. Employees should also know and understand the performance review system the company uses. Performance Reviews are an opportunity for building a stronger working relationship and improving communication with the staff and from the point of view of the employee it may be a chance to get clarity, assess training needs and future career options.

Review meetings have to be planned and set at a time which is the least disruptive for normal work to ensure full engagement and attention. Both parties should prepare in advance and go to the meeting with a clear idea of what the desired outcome is. The manager should start in a positive tone to get the right atmosphere, explain the objectives of the meeting, where appropriate, and list the employee's achievements in the period. He should then ask if there are any that he has missed. A Performance Review is a conversation, not a lecture where the manager is doing all the talking. This will make the employee feel defensive and not take proper notice of the areas where improvement is necessary.

If supervisors and managers are doing a good job, nothing should come as a surprise to the employees. Performance issues should have been pointed out as they have occurred and information given on what should have been done instead. It is important to keep written records of all relevant conversations to track the evolution of the employee's performance. This review must cover the whole period, not only recent events which can distort the judgment on the employees' performance.

Listening to the employees is essential because it is an opportunity for both parties to make things work better. Employees should be asked what they want and need, what they feel proud of or concerned about. The gaps that are identified during the reviews should originate clear and timely corrective action plans. If the organization has supported the employee with adequate training and supervision and the goals were not met, there will have to be consequences which the employee is already expecting.

Performance reviews enhance employee-manager communication and increase performance in the organization because they raise the need to work on any issues throughout the year. The notes from the Review and the agreed action plan will be a roadmap to ensure that goals and expectations for the next period are met.

68 Improving Salary and Benefits Package

The purpose of a balanced compensation plan is to attract, retain and motivate the best people. To accomplish these goals, companies use a mixture of base pay (salary), incentive pay (cash or non-cash awards such as stock) and benefits (non-financial rewards). The mix of these three components is important and varies from industry to industry. A company may decide to offer salaries above market value and not worry too much about incentives and benefits if the commercial component is weak and average salaries in the industry are low.

Pay should take into consideration both proficiency and performance. Proficiency rates the employees' skills compared to their peers in the organization and industry. Performance looks at how the employees behave in relation to what was expected from them.

As employees become proficient in their jobs, it is important to move to the next level so they don't feel they stagnate in functions and pay. This can reduce motivation and the best search for a challenge elsewhere. Although compensation practices should be consistent, not discriminative or arbitrary, they may contemplate different approaches for different types of jobs to cover circumstances where a position is difficult to fill or crucial to the bottom line. All senior management must be involved in determining the compensation plans so they align it with the company's objectives and vision.

Incentives were once a privilege of management and the sales force, but with the change in economic conditions a lot of large and small companies have adopted incentive plans for all their staff that combine individual and overall performance. Incentive payments show appreciation and link individual performance to the company's results.

Profit-sharing plans may reduce staff turnover but can be a problem in a more volatile economy. The perceived value of these plans has decreased because the economic value is too volatile and dependent on factors outside the employee's control. Employees who achieve extraordinary accomplishment should also receive a one-time bonus.

A well-designed incentive-pay plan can be an important tool to steer employees' efforts and attention to the immediate priorities, thus providing a quick way to course correct the company's performance. Some employee benefits are required by law namely different types of insurance cover (Social Security, unemployment and workers' compensation). Others are optional, like health insurance including dental plan, pensions, various types of paid leaves, retirement-savings plan, etc. If the company offers a competitive benefits package that fits the target employees' needs it will contribute to increase job satisfaction and decrease turnover.

Research shows that above a certain salary level that covers the basic needs, money does not constitute a strong, ongoing reward in itself. Workers expect to be valued as human beings, so one of the primary rewards is often feeling a sense of meaning or purpose in their work. A common complaint from employees is that they don't feel appreciated. Fostering employee development by tuition reimbursement on areas deemed useful but not available in the organization may be important.

Small perks like free coffee and bagels or dry-cleaning pickup and delivery may seem insignificant but can be greatly appreciated by some. Other benefits like sports or social clubs can be important because physical exercise and social activities improve health and reduce stress, also contributing to team building and improving communication in the organization. It all depends on how many people actually participate and the value they attach to these activities.

Communication of customers' positive comments, a direct compliment from the 'boss' or public acknowledgement in staff meetings is cheap and works as well as other paid incentives. Increased responsibility, flexible schedules and additional time off can be rewards in themselves.

Regular reviews of incentives and benefits need to be made because the perception of their value changes over time and the company must be sure they are spending the money wisely. The important thing is that employees realize that they are being rewarded not just for working hard but for generating results for the company.

69 High Staff Turnover

Employee turnover is expensive for an organization. Various estimates suggest that losing a middle manager costs an organization up to 100% of his annual salary. The loss of a senior executive is even more costly.

The organization's capacity to engage, retain, and optimize the value of its employees hinges on how well jobs are designed and how well employees are matched to the needs and values of the organization - an organization should not hire or keep any staff member that doesn't play a role in its mission.

Top management needs to closely monitor factors that affect staff turnover rates. These include selection, induction, development, matching jobs to people (both skills and aspirations), appraisals, compensation, career evolution and relationship with managers. Occasional health or personal issues also have to be identified. Obviously, the major factors for staff leaving should be identified and corrected first.

When the turnover is high it can also affect the morale, reduce the productivity of the staff and the quality of the products and services because of the increase in stress levels, interruptions to the work flow and missed deadlines. This is especially the case when those who leave played a key role in the success or continuity of the organization, so retaining staff and treating them fairly to assure continuity and stability has to be part of your business's culture.

Engaged employees are passionate about the work they do and committed to achieving the strategic goals for the business. The Gallup Organization has proven that engaged employees are more productive, customer-focused and likely to resist temptations to leave (their study has shown that organizations with high levels of employee engagement post 2.6 times the growth rate in earnings per share compared with other organizations in the same industry).

Managers need to be trained and supported in dealing with any disciplinary or grievance procedures and ensure they give their staff adequate and regular feedback on their performance. It is always a good investment to have an on-going program to constantly improve your management's leadership and team building skills. They will feel good about their development and contribution to the business and that will impact the way they help drive the business forward, and develop other workers.

Pay is very seldom the only reason why people leave, although if compensation is below a certain level, it makes it almost impossible for employees to stay. The quality of the supervision an employee receives is critical to employee retention. People leave managers and supervisors more often than companies or jobs. Frequent employee complaints center on lack of clarity about expectations, earning potential, lack of feedback about performance and failure to provide a framework within which the employee perceives he can succeed.

Involving the staff by informing them of what is going on in the company, creating open communication between employees and management, holding regular meetings in which employees can offer ideas and ask questions and having an open-door policy that encourages everyone to speak frankly with their managers without fear of repercussion will make employees feel part of the organization.

A team-work and a no-blame philosophy will also result in a more proactive approach to problem solving. Trusting employees by giving them more control over their work can also be a powerful motivator and a reason to stay.

The perception of fairness and equitable treatment is important in employee retention. Your staff members must feel rewarded, recognized and appreciated. Creating the culture and conditions for the best employees will ensure customer satisfaction, product sales, satisfied co-workers and a stronger base for growth and effective succession planning.

70 Lack of Good Staff

'Lack of Good Staff' is a complaint you often hear from business owners either referring to their business or to somebody else's usually when they are not happy with the service they are providing. This can be because there are no people available with the skills that they need, or that there are none willing to join at the salaries being offered.

Is there a case for rethinking where the business is recruiting from?

LinkedIn or some other online platform is sometimes an effective option to contact the right people. If the skills needed are very specific, then either in-house training or an agreement with a local college could be a solution. Poaching from competitors may get you the staff you need but their loyalty may be an issue. Hence you could lose them just as easily as you got them.

Some employers neglect the importance of matching correctly the person to the job and the organization. Changing the perspective from 'good candidates' and 'bad candidates' to 'candidates that fit the job' and 'those who don't' would keep them from recruiting someone overqualified or with the wrong profile for the job just because they came across great in the interview. A bad fit will sooner or later become a poor performer no matter how good they look on paper.

The company needs to have a comprehensive people strategy and a well-structured recruiting program to ensure they make the right match when recruiting. Job descriptions should reflect the roles the individual will fill, the skill sets and personality attributes needed and any prior experience needed. This information should be reviewed for each recruitment to make sure all elements still apply and that there are none missing. Knowing exactly what you are looking for will help the screening process - only interview candidates that match the profile.

In the interview, it is advisable to use similar questions to ensure you are evaluating candidates consistently. Sometimes it is useful to use a proven assessment tool. Use the information collected to adjust compensation (within the pre-determined range) for the candidate selected and also as a base to develop his or her training program.

Supply and demand in the job market are not linear. Most times it is not just about the salary package. Commute distances, working atmosphere, career plan, training and job security all form part of the equation in some way or another. A poor salary package can still attract staff in hard times but as soon as the conditions change employees will leave unless there is a great work atmosphere, training and career plans.

Several of my restaurant clients here in Portugal complain they can't hire or keep good staff. Portuguese employees are reluctant to work evenings and weekends and Brazilian staff can be unreliable (taking time off and leaving without giving notice). Tight margins mean it is hard to pay extra to attract the Portuguese and increasing the assiduity of the Brazilian staff is also difficult. Annual bonus is too far out in the future. Monthly or quarterly bonus work better, but they have to be enough to keep them, but not so large that the moment they receive it they go back to Brazil on holiday.

One solution that had an impact on the Portuguese staff was to give vouchers for 20€ off an evening meal for two if they worked the unpopular shifts. This could be used by friends or family and although it had no immediate cash impact for the business it had a good perceived value for the staff with far less cost to the restaurants.

An 'outside the box' solution may go a long way in getting and keeping the right staff. There may be 'difficult jobs' because they involve unpleasant working conditions, demand a lot in physical, intellectual or emotional terms. However, there are always people who are prepared to do them and even get satisfaction from it. It is about perspective and finding the right person. The right supervision, quality feedback and recognition are critical for good performance. Exit interviews provide valuable information on what can be done to keep staff happy, productive and providing clients the quality experience they deserve.

71 Improving Leadership

Today's organizations need their leaders to be almost super-humans! They have to possess a long list of business skills in finance, cost control, resource allocation, product development, marketing, manufacturing, technology, etc. and also master the management arts - strategy, motivation, persuasion, negotiation, active listening, speaking, presenting and writing. In addition, they are supposed to take responsibility for organizational success, generate profits and share them generously while demonstrating the qualities that define leadership, integrity and character - vision, fortitude, commitment, passion, sensitivity, insight, intelligence, ethical standards, charisma, resilience, courage and humility. Ideally they should also be friends, mentors or guardians and on perpetually alert to defend all stakeholders best interests.

Most schools and universities have been unable to adapt to the new paradigms in business and society. They have been unable to predict the economy trends and they concentrate the curricula on strategy issues, disregarding implementation. They also tend to focus most of their attention on technical aspects, forgetting to develop interpersonal and relationship skills.

Successful organizations need leaders at all levels to inspire others to perform at their best level in the pursuit of the organization's goals. Without leadership people do not have the energy or motivation to do what needs to be done and productivity and performance suffer. Leaders engaging in the old management-by-exception style, who don't intervene until problems are either brought to their attention or become serious enough to demand action, can compromise the organization's performance with their passive attitude.

Lack of leadership skills may also be a source of stress for both the manager (who does not have the right competences) and for his or her subordinates. This is why it is so important to have a well-designed leadership training program for the whole organization.

Leadership can be taught by helping the employees to discover the power that lies within them to make a difference so that they assume their share of responsibility in making a positive impact in the results of the organization. To have effective leadership you also need to have effective communication, vision and clarity. If a leader doesn't care about his job, neither will the members of his team. If the leader is confused about direction, frustration will soak into the layers below.

However, if the roles of each person are clearly identified, with authority and accountability clearly stated, the leader's commitment will permeate throughout all levels of the organization, engaging middle and front-line leaders. By assigning well-defined roles and fostering creativity, growth and effective feedback in the organization all individuals will be able to succeed and take pride in their achievements.

Concurrently, trust and recognition will allow information to travel upwards in the hierarchy and management will be more attuned to the reality of what is going on and be able to react quickly to problems before they escalate to unmanageable proportions. An organization where all employees are aligned with the mission and values, and take pride in working as a team, will be able to provide great products and services and attract and maintain the best customers in the market.

72 Improving Team-Work

> *"Coming together is a beginning. Keeping together is progress. Working together is success."*
> *Henry Ford*

A team is a group of people with complementary skills for a desired outcome who support each other and hold themselves mutually accountable in the process of achieving the specific result they are committed to.

One of the characteristics of a great team is the collaborative atmosphere. Each member brings their best ideas to the table confident that the others will listen and other team members will formulate even more powerful ideas. It is about constantly exchanging, refining and combining ideas, leading to more successful and profitable ways of doing business.

Team building is essential in any organization. It is more than about the ability of each member of the staff to work and perform together. It is about the fact that a good team is capable of much more than the sum of the capacity of its individuals. Team work leverages the talent and competencies of its members and can work magic if there is trust and team spirit amongst the members.

Many organizations invest time and money in events that supposedly help team members bond and function coherently by learning about each other's behavioral styles, motivational profiles, individual strengths, etc. However, sometimes the results are not the best if the organizers fail to show how to channel team behavior to achieve business results. Individuals who are accustomed to operating independently will not see the value of operating as a whole. Other times there is no follow-up beyond the one-time event and the message is immediately lost when people get sucked back into their old daily routines.

Working for an organization is belonging to a team that has the same mission and common goals. Committed members of the staff from the top management to the office boy should feel part of something larger than themselves because they feel that their values are aligned with the values, mission and objectives of the organization and that is having a positive impact in the world. This is part of the 'us' feeling but it is not enough to produce efficient teamwork.

Teams should always be working for the best possible outcome and be flexible about adopting new procedures or new approaches. The most effective teams follow best practices but are quick to adapt to environment or organizational changes as they operate based on open and constructive communication and mutual trust, working for the best results for the company instead of their individual agendas.

In some organizations employees are unable to work as a team because they don't really know how to function – they may have lost focus on the results they want to achieve, or they have never been clear on their goals in the first place. In this case they often make assumptions, become judgmental, speculate or point fingers. Individuals react to circumstances and there's no strategic focus or energy to move forward. Team building can also backfire due to over competitive behavior.

The leader must step in and clarify the goals and expectations and ask the team members to individually articulate their understanding of the overall goals in their own words. The whole team should assign tasks and determine how progress and results are going to be monitored.

Leadership is critical to help the team to succeed and stay together building trust and leveraging each member's strengths. In a team-oriented environment each employee contributes to the overall success of the organization. Each person works to produce results. Even though each member of the staff has a specific function and belongs to a specific department, they are unified with other organization members to accomplish the overall objectives. The bigger picture drives the actions, not the department's interests or individual agendas.

Building great teamwork within a corporation leads to building great teamwork between the company and their customers and drives better business results.

Main Takeaways:

1.

2.

3.

Improvements to implement:

Action 1.

By: Start Date: Ready by:

Action 2.

By: Start Date: Ready by:

Action 3.

By: Start Date: Ready by:

Finance

"Numbers rule the universe"
Pythagoras

The Finance function is much more than keeping track of the money. Finance activities include Accounting and Reporting, Financial Control (setting internal control policies, reconciling external statements and monitoring payment of invoices), Compliance (meeting governmental and other regulatory bodies' requirements), Management and Control (preparation of financial and related information to inform, monitor and support operational actions to meet organizational objectives), Strategy and Risk Management and Funding (assess, negotiate and obtain the financial resources that the organization needs).

The survival of the organization in today's competitive environment depends largely on the quality and timely delivery of financial information to management, stakeholders and regulatory bodies.

In **www.BusinessGrothLevers.com/resources** you will find some schedules to support you in planning and controlling Finance.

73 Accountant's Competence Level

Accountants are responsible for preparing financial statements in a timely manner to assist management in making proper decisions.

However, management needs to understand what the statements are really portraying. Occasionally managers will refuse to admit they don't understand the data and will ignore important information, just filing reports without studying them.

If accountants take the time to sit down with management and explain what is being presented and highlight problem areas – clients that are not paying or products' sales that are declining or not following the usual pattern – they could even assist in providing the necessary data to pinpoint the underlying issues and possible corrective measures.

Additionally accountants could assist management in funding negotiations by preparing the data in such a way that would facilitate the process with the lending institution.

Finally, it is the accountant's responsibility to inform the business owner of new accounting standards and regulations which affect the activity or the figures (some changes in accounting procedures may affect the presentation so the figures for different periods will not be comparable).

If accounting is being outsourced you must be very careful choosing the right professional, since he or she must have qualifications, experience and knowledge of your type of business. There are different procedures, rules and regulations for different businesses and it is a big challenge to keep up with everything. Surveys show that some small businesses fall prey of incompetent accountants (some who even misrepresent their skills and background) or, more commonly, indifferent accountants, who may be qualified but just crunch the numbers without providing any further information or assistance.

Not having an in-house accountant leaves business owners more exposed to bad advice by 'well meaning' friends. For example, some small businesses think it is a good idea to finance their operation through the use of payroll taxes! Internal or external accountants must stress the importance of compliance with all regulations to ensure the continuity of the business.

A common mistake business owners make that accountants should help them avoid is mixing their money and the corporations. Owners sometimes use the company's funds for personal expenses or as 'loans' and vice versa without clear documentation. This can create financing difficulties and tax problems both for them as individuals and for the business. Accountants have to make sure that clients understand the importance of keeping their accounts separate from the business for financial reporting and payroll tax purposes.

Finally it is important to understand that for the accountant to have time to really assist the business owner in the different areas the fee has to reflect the time spent. If the fee is low the accountant will have to reduce the extent of the service or even compromise its quality.

74 Improving Internal Controls

Internal controls exist to protect assets, reduce risks and ensure reliable reporting. In difficult economic times, where companies are closing down and people being laid off every day, there is a higher probability of fraud and theft from inside and outside the company. Both can have lethal effect on the health of the business.

It is difficult for small businesses to have segregation of duties due to insufficient employees. However tasks should be divided between people to reduce risk of the error or inappropriate actions. No one person should be able to control all aspects of any financial transaction. You cannot have the same person write checks, reconcile the accounts and even go to the bank. This would be a weakness in the internal controls since that person would have access to an asset and be able to tamper with the recording of the transaction to conceal the fraud.

Make sure all relevant transactions (in terms of value and overall impact on the business) are authorized by the owner, CEO or someone with written authority. Records need to be periodically reviewed and reconciled, by someone other than those who prepare them or are involved in the transaction. Equipment, inventories, cash and other assets should be secured physically, counted periodically and the results reconciled with the records.

In very small businesses the owners may receive bank statements themselves and have someone open the mail and keep a log of what comes in to avoid checks or statements 'getting lost'. When accounting is outsourced collections and payments should stay in-house or be outsourced to another entity to avoid problems.

All staff should be trained in the procedures and have easy access to the manuals so that day-to-day operations run smoothly even in the event of employee absences. Policies and procedures should be reviewed regularly to ascertain whether results are consistent with established objectives and employees should be encouraged to make suggestions for improvement.

Businesses that have been established for some time may have excessive manual processing and a higher potential for human error. There are multiple software options (either owned or rented in the 'cloud' for a reasonable monthly fee) for most accounting activities. A complete transaction can be sequenced and approved in the system and this can involve different levels of staff in the office or outside (using mobile devices). The investment in such a solution might be compensated by a reduction of time and cost making reconciliations.

Implementation of accounting and internal control best practices together with adequate technology for your business size and activity can significantly reduce the workload. Additionally it can improve accuracy, response time, qu2ality and employee motivation. It will also ensure compliance with laws and regulations, improve accuracy of the financial data and reporting and be more cost efficient.

If a business has written internal controls and procedures that prevent, quickly detect and correct problems the quality and reliability of the information is higher, management will be able to make better decisions and you will gain stakeholders' confidence.

75 Financial Plan/Budget

More and more I hear business owners say "I don't know how things might go over the next year, so why waste time on a financial plan and a budget?" Just because they may have missed the budget completely in the current period it does not mean budgeting is a waste of time!

This all ties in with whether you run your business or it is your business that is running you…

Making a plan requires that you examine the business and think about what has and hasn't worked up to now and how you can improve in the future. It is an exercise that gives you a chance to think systematically, analyze different scenarios and redefine or adjust goals.

Using the prior year figures to show the trend from the same month in the prior year is a start if there are seasonal fluctuations in your business. However, all other variables that are affecting the market and your organization at present plus your 'take' on the trends should be factored in to adjust this starting point.

An alternative, where there is little seasonality, is to take the total for the prior year, apply the growth factor required and divide by 12 to get a monthly goal, or to project forward the trends for the prior year. This can be used for rolling budgets, just adding another month at a time, but it is only the beginning of the process.

It is important that you start to get some numbers that can be used as points of reference. As the business grows the budget process should evolve into an integrated approach including Profit and Loss, Balance

Sheet and Cash Flow with Headcount, Capital Expenditure, Marketing and other budgets as needed. Priorities can be established based on the factors that will hold the company back if not addressed.

A good spreadsheet model will link all of the budgets so that any adjustment made in one place will reflect throughout the whole budget. For example changing Sales automatically changes Inventory, Accounts Receivable, Cash Flow and Financing needs. "What if" scenarios can be tested and pessimistic, optimistic or most likely outcomes evaluated.

Two methods of preparing the budget using the prior year results as a starting point are the 'Top Down' and the 'Bottom Up' approaches.

Another method is the 'Zero Based Budgeting' where each line of the budget is scrutinized and has to be justified. This is more time consuming but goes farther towards the most efficient allocation of resources and cutting waste.

As a business grows, responsibility for revenue and expenses will have to be delegated. Good communication and a deep understanding of the company's mission and its goals and objectives will facilitate the process. Well prepared budgets will reduce stress because they show where the business is and where it needs to go. They are also an excellent tool to measure performance.

There are a variety of reasons why you might not know how the business is really doing in financial terms: lack of quality and/or timely financial information, poor segregation between the business finances and yours, poor time management, etc. A very common reason is lack of understanding of finance and this can be fixed very easily through a personalized training program, seeking help from a business coach or mentor and at a more advanced stage joining a Mastermind Group (where peers help each other to grow their businesses).

'A good businessman knows the numbers, a great businessman understands them'
Unknown

76 Accounting Deficiencies

The purpose of Accounting is to record the financial impact of business activities. Records are based on charts of accounts and enable the production of trial balances, profit and loss statements and balance sheets once accounts are checked and reconciled. This information is invaluable for management, banks and other stakeholders.

What do you do with your accounts? Are they just for the fiscal authorities and to prepare the annual report or are you using them to actually manage the business?

The first obstacle is often that the accounts are not up to date. The time it takes for the accountant to receive and check all the data and then produce monthly results will depend on the volume of documents, number of staff and degree of automation and integration. The most efficient is a paperless system with all documents either produced by the system, or scanned in. If the accounting is all on-line, then it is only the time needed to reconcile some accounts (like banks), and to process any adjustments and the monthly figures will be ready soon after the month ends.

The second obstacle is the complexity of the business, number of locations, business lines and cost centers. Data needs to be reliable so there have to be clearly defined rules to ensure consistent procedures are followed. For example if electricity invoices are received every other month, a monthly provision has to be made based on estimates, with subsequent corrections if significant, so that monthly results are accurate.

Outsourcing, using an external accountant, may be needed for a small company without the volume of business to justify the cost of an in-house accountant. The drawbacks are there may be delays as the external accountant probably has other customers who take priority, information may not be in the best format and documents might have to physically leave the premises.

Make sure you get your complete data to the external accountant as early as possible so they can have your figures ready on time.

It is important to have a written agreement with the accountant as to timings both for your staff to deliver the data and for the accountant to produce the figures. If you are late delivering data he may have to work late and under stress and should be compensated. If you deliver everything as agreed and he doesn't get your financials done on time then there should be a reduction in the fee for the following month and he should pick up any penalties for late filings.

Timely and accurate financial data is indispensable for running the business. Often external accountants will merely process the documents and data they receive without checking it for completeness. In this case the information provided can be useless and you would need an in-house system to process at least some of the information, which would be duplication and a waste of money.

If you use an external accountant he can have a systems to control the accuracy of some of the information you provide, like making sure regular recurring items (i.e. rent and utilities) are accounted for each month. However other items, unless they are large, don't always stand out so you have to make sure that information on all transactions gets sent and registered.

77 Inadequate Analysis

There can be many reasons why financial results differ from the objectives and a good manager will go deep into finding the explanations of these variations. Sometimes there is the temptation to go for the easy answer but often there are factors that partly or totally cancel each other out and mask the impact of the real issues. At other times it is a problem with poor control of the accuracy of the information that was recorded.

Is spending on salaries over budget due to overtime, more staff hired than budgeted, holiday pay not apportioned over the year or an exceptional one-time payment like a lay-off?

Normally variations are either price or quantity (sometimes known as volume). If you are in manufacturing, then the raw materials might cost more, or for a variety of reasons the amount used could be higher. Reasons can include extra wastage due to poor quality of raw materials, machine problems or less experienced employees. There may also be theft, obsolescence, poor storage and handling or a mixture. For example in the past the usage of paper in newspaper printing increased when the weather was damp as the paper had a higher tendency to break when going through the press at high speeds. Better presses, paper quality, storage conditions and less stock reduced this problem.

Proper analysis requires a good understanding of the business, an inquisitive and analytical mind plus some 'detective work' to unravel complex situations.

When looking at variations it is important to bear in mind what assumptions were used in the budget and whether it was realistic, optimistic or pessimistic. Setting a budget that is unrealistic in both price and quantity will result in large variations as the quantity is multiplied by the price.

Depending on the size and complexity of the business the analysis may be done by yourself, an assistant or by someone in finance. Being good with numbers is important but communication skills are a big plus to get correct information on time. Bringing together the data across departments and helping department heads understand their results can be time consuming but provide huge benefits for teamwork.

Transversal information should be supplied by the appropriate department, for example headcount figures come from the HR department so no employees fall through the cracks and there is a consistent basis.

If the Budget isn't linked to the accounting, then the progress can't be so easily measured. There are various software accounting packages that allow integration of budgets and customizable reports. Provided there is a spreadsheet framework developed that matches the format of the accounting reports, the budget figures can be directly imported. It is important to check the integrity of the figures, especially if there are complex allocations, to ensure no cost centers are missed.

Budgets often have numerous revisions and adjustments. Make sure that it is the final version that is used for the reporting.

78 Looking Beyond the Numbers

What if you have a quick glance at the numbers and they look good? Does that mean everything is under control and business is thriving? Can we just smile, put them in a file and forget about them? We might have a surprise if we were to drill down and look at the figures in detail. Sometimes figures just give a snapshot, but not the trend, plus they can be distorted by an exceptional item.

The following example relates to a small photocopier reseller with 3 key accounts where the sales for the month were 59,000. Apparently this is great because it is 3,000 over budget. When the breakdown is checked, the detail tells a different story.

	Budget	**Actual**
Client A	15,000	30,000
Client B	6,000	0
Client C	6,000	0
Miscellaneous Sales	29,000	29,000
Total	**56,000**	**59,000**

The question that jumps off the page is why B and C didn't buy anything?

Are there orders in the pipeline for next month, were there inventory issues, have we lost them as customers (and if so why?) or did the salesman not have time to visit them (sickness, holidays, training etc.)?

On the other hand, the excellent results for A have to be taken with caution and in the right perspective.

Was there a delay in shipping from the prior month, will they maintain this level of business next month, or was there something else extraordinary in some way this particular month?

How is Client A in terms of their credit limit - is there a significant risk and a potential impact on cash-flow?

Did he get volume discounts or is he buying a product mix that will reduce the profit margin?

If sales to Client A are really going well, then you need to know how those sales are being achieved, so that it can be duplicated with other customers.

The next step is to take a look at the sales team and their commissions. Is someone going hungry, perhaps not making their house or car payments, and hence weighed down by personal problems that have stressed them out so they can't sell effectively?

How is the team's motivation? How are sales split between them?

There is a lot of other important data missing besides the impact of these results on margins and cash flow. Inventory levels may be low which will affect sales for the following month(s), only one model might be selling, spare parts could be in short supply, maintenance staff may not have been trained for new machine yet etc.

Understanding the numbers is essential for the success of the business but they only point the direction you should follow to investigate what is wrong or could be improved. The big secret is to focus on the key indicators that are crucial for each business and not getting bogged down in insignificant detail. The key indicators depend on the activity, size of the business, growth stage, etc. and should be a mix that covers the key areas of the company.

Remember the Pareto principle – often 20% of the products are responsible for 80% of the margin, 20% of the clients generate 80% of the revenue… so look for the most relevant data that can show you the problem areas before your business is seriously affected.

A business needs to be seen as a whole. Identify trends, potential problems and appropriate solutions so that the business keeps moving in the right direction and serving the clients beyond their expectations.

79 Finding the right KPIs

In simple terms a KPI (Key Performance Indicator) is a means to measuring how well a company or business units is performing compared to the strategic goals and objectives.

Generic KPIs may not be the best for your business. Although businesses in the same industry sector have generally similar survival objectives, the operational differences and specific strategic goals may mean that they need KPIs tailored for what they are trying to achieve.

If a company's goal is to increase market penetration or geographic reach, it might want to measure KPIs around the orders pipeline. If the business wants to attract and keep customers by creating a great brand, it might measure brand awareness and customer satisfaction. If staff turnover has become a problem, monitor recruitment efficiency, feedback on training or compensation plans versus the competition.

There are many KPIs to choose from and the biggest challenge for a company is to select the right ones at that particular moment in time. Bad choice of KPIs will keep management focused in the wrong issues and will result in them missing information that would have enabled them to react to events that can significantly impact the business.

Since KPIs need to originate from the businesses mission and goals, a good place to start is to revisit the objectives that are critical for the survival of the business. Truly understanding the business means knowing what benefits it really offers to the customers and how this can be done and improved in a cost effective, efficient way. Knowledge of the competition and market trends is also important. In the current market conditions, unless management knows exactly what they want to accomplish it is going to be difficult to design the best strategy and the KPIs that will help monitor its implementation progress.

It is important to choose KPIs that relate to aspects of your business that you can control. Monitoring the price of a raw material is of little relevance compared to measuring the impact that the variations will have on the business's margins.

Some KPIs are usually linked to the high level goals of the business like return on investment, profit margin, sales figures, customer complaints, etc. but it is the additional KPIs you choose that are unique to your business that will make the difference.

What is the best way of measuring your performance and progress towards your business goals?

Which objectives are considered by the staff to be more relevant? Here, depending on the size of the business, you can have department KPIs (needless to say they have to be aligned with the big picture) or one integrated set for the whole business.

KPIs help clarifying, keeping track of organizational performance, profitability and productivity levels. By monitoring the progress against forecasts management can make adjustments based on figures instead of 'feelings' or guesswork.

80 Confusion between Profit and Cash Flow

Because of the recession and the difficulty in getting financing businesses are more aware of cash flow than ever. However, for a business to be successful it has to have an adequate cash balance plus healthy profit figures. Cash is a need, but real profit is a must since no business can survive if it is not economically viable.

For a large number of small business owners the difference between Profit and Cash flow is unclear hence bad decisions are made. Cash flow is the money that flows in and out from operations, financing activities, and investing activities. Profit is the mathematical difference between sales revenue and all costs and expenses regardless of when payments are made or collections received.

One of the main reasons for the difference between cash and profit figures is the dissimilarity in timing between when products or services are sold or bought and the cash is received or paid.

It is possible for a company to be profitable but have little or no cash. Contributing factors could be having to paying suppliers up front (no credit), investing in equipment without financing, repaying loans or, most commonly selling on extended credit terms.

In this case the business needs money from a financial institution or the shareholders. If no money is available the company may not be able to continue operations and will be profitable but broke. If a loan is obtained, the interest and charges will reduce the profits.

It is possible for a business to be cash rich but unprofitable. This happens often to businesses that pay suppliers on credit but have cash sales. There will be surplus cash as long as sales keep growing

Another two factors to be considered are inventory and investment. If the business keeps a high level of stock it will not affect the profit because you only account for the cost of the goods sold when you sell them but it will impact your cash flow immediately or within the term you have negotiated with your supplier for the payment. As for Investments in equipment or vehicles, the impact on Cash Flow will be when the payment is made but in terms of Profit it will be spread monthly over the life of the asset (depreciation).

All businesses must have cash budgets based on the objectives for the year but also prepare monthly cash forecasts to make sure the cash flowing into the business is enough to keep it going. Unfortunately there are clients that never pay because they go out of business… In this case was there ever a real sale? The revenue will disappear and the profit will become a loss.

Forecasting and monitoring cash flow is a great way to red flag clients that delay payments and make sure they are put on credit hold quickly.

Sustained success is totally dependent on consistent, positive cash flow from operations resulting from healthy profitable operations that allow for the business to be run smoothly.

81 Lack of Capital

Before the economic downturn it was easy for small businesses that had an ongoing relationship with a bank to get at least a line of credit. During the last years the markets have become more competitive, businesses have lost customers, had reduced profits and assets have lost value, which affected their creditworthiness. On the other hand banks have tightened their lending guidelines.

Until a business can support its financing needs through building up a cash surplus it will need new capital, loans or some very understanding suppliers to grow.

Over borrowing is one of the biggest causes of business failure. A lot of businesses are unable to meet repayments of capital and interest on loans as they become due. If your existing business isn't generating enough surplus cash to make repayments on a loan then you need to look at increasing capital or review the business model.

To get new investors, or a bank loan, the ratio between capital and liabilities is important. Capital comes from the shares issued, retained profits or some types of shareholder loans.

Lack of capital can impact the willingness of others to invest or lend money and the rates of interest or conditions that they require. If the business is under-capitalized, then you may be asked to give personal guarantees such as a second mortgage on your home or a life insurance policy. If you have other personal assets then banks will question why you want to use their money instead of your own and to compensate them for taking more risk than you they increase their interest charges.

If you don't have enough faith in your business to risk your own money then why should a bank?

If you opt for finding an investor and he wants shares in the company, you will have to weigh the benefit of the additional cash against the possible loss of control. It is wise to weight all pros and cons like how much knowledge/experience, contacts or synergies will the investor be bringing to the businesses

There is often a temptation when the business suddenly has a large sale or surplus cash to buy a new car, take a bonus or a vacation. It is also a temptation when a business loan works out cheaper than a personal loan. This is a huge mistake that has got a lot of small businesses into trouble. Money evaporates or is used for high depreciation assets instead of being kept to avoid borrowing in the future when new fixed assets were needed.

Generally speaking, another major cause of small businesses failure is the difficulty owners have in keeping the businesses' funds separated from their own money and the fact they keep on using the businesses' money for personal purposes. This creates confusion as to the real Cash Flow and profitability of the business, masks the trends and can restrain future growth.

The more share capital and retained earnings a company has, the less it is exposed to economic downturns or pressure from banks or outside investors.

82 Badly Structured Funding

Banks need tangible assets as backing for loans with a preference for property that holds its' value and equipment that can easily be sold, like vehicles.

If you can get a loan, the value of the asset used for the guarantee needs to be greater than the amount of the loan. Obviously financial institutions want to reduce the risk of losing their money in the case of default and allow for any reduction in value of the asset in the case of a forced or quick sale.

If a loan is for a short period and the bank wants an asset like a building as guarantee, it then becomes more complicated to use the building as security for other loans. Hence the need to match long term assets with long term loans to give more stability to the funding of the business. Where possible a relationship needs to be built with lenders to avoid frequent renegotiation and uncertainty.

Locking-in interest rates for as long as possible reduces uncertainty but banks will insist on higher rates. Let's face it, they are in business to make money so they increase the rate to cover all risks and may be reluctant to fix rates for more than a few months when there are large fluctuations in the capital markets.

Will the business be able to generate enough cash to repay the loan, or is the idea to roll the loan over?

If there is a strong possibility that there will be the need to roll the loan over it is better to try and negotiate a longer term up front in case conditions change and the bank doesn't want to renew the loan.

If the loan is needed to buy an asset with a long life, for example a building, a long term loan with regular repayments will facilitate planning and take the pressure off cash flow. If it is the case of some expensive equipment or vehicles (say trucks or vans) the same applies.

Long term loans are usually cheaper than leasing but if the term does not match the expected life of the asset, leasing may be a valid option.

There is a tendency to rent premises rather than buying based on the assumption that the business will soon need more space or needs to be flexible. This may be true for many businesses, however, owning the premises will improve the financial stability of the business (provided the property holds its value) and if the business needs to move the premises can always be sold or rented out. Over a long enough period, well located and good quality property normally appreciates in value and is usually the preferred type of collateral for most types of loans.

There are usually other costs of arranging loans such as valuations, fees and taxes, besides the time taken in negotiations and paperwork. The shorter the period of the loan, the more frequently these costs will be incurred.

83 Not Enough Cash

How much could you save if you had more money available?

Would suppliers give you a better price or discount if you made payment earlier?

Do you have to pay interest charges and penalties because of overdue payments?

How about missing out on good deals like volume discounts or special offers?

This is the tangible side of the lack of cash. The intangible costs are stress, wasting time and energy trying to juggle cash flow and possible deterioration of relationships with customers, suppliers and even staff. If you have trouble making the payroll, the word is likely to spread quickly that you are in trouble. Suddenly you may find banks withdrawing credit lines and suppliers asking for payment up front.

Tight control of expenses can avoid wasting money and improve profits. A saving in expenses gives an immediate benefit while a saving in product cost only helps when you make a sale.

Over time bad habits can set in, especially in grey areas that are cross functional. Here are some suggestions:

Rent - what are current rates in the area? Renegotiate a lower rent or reduced space. Staff often spread out to fill the space.

Electricity - is the building kept too warm in the winter and too cool in the summer? Ensure lights are turned off when not needed and equipment is not left on standby for long periods - weekends or holidays. Would more energy efficient lights/equipment bring savings?

Communication - are non-urgent items being sent by courier that could be normal post or at overnight rates? Do staff pay for personal usage of company mobile phones? Are all phones accounted for or have people left and kept a phone or card that you are paying for?

Printing/copying - switching to 100% paperless is not an easy option, but usually considerable savings can be made. Is the right machine in the right place? Would swapping old machines for new more efficient models bring savings? Think before you print!

Outsourced Services - periodically these should be evaluated to ensure you are getting value for money. An external service provider, like an accountant or cleaner might go the extra mile the first year but then increase rates or lower the level of service. Meet with them and ask how you can work together to reduce fees. With accounting it might be some simple clerical work, like preparation of summaries or batching documents that can be done in-house at little or no cost. With cleaning it could be asking staff to leave their work area tidy so cleaning can be done quicker and more efficiently.

Insurance - regular reviews of policies by an experienced broker can result in savings as well as ensuring coverage is adequate.

Office supplies, etc. - centralized purchasing can bring savings by finding the best suppliers and rates. Having one person with overall responsibility increases ownership and accountability. Drawbacks are difficulty controlling multi-locations and the time spent on small gains.

Delaying payment to suppliers is common practice. Some CFOs have devised systems to delay paying and track excuses made to each Supplier (including the classic 'the check in the post', 'forgetting' to sign checks or deliberately swapping envelopes so two suppliers get each other's checks).

In situations like this it is not about getting discounts or better deals, it is about survival. Your business can be at risk due to reduction in the quality of the products or services you are getting or you may be unable to honor your commitments due to a supply interruption from one of your vendors. Unfortunately too many companies are in trouble and these practices have a snow ball effect on the economy.

84 Poor Credit Control

The rate of change in the global economy has increased so much that a healthy company can find itself in trouble in a very short space of time.

Tight control over current expenses is important but management has to reduce financial risk on all fronts to keep the business healthy.

In some industries new products are launched very quickly and no one wants obsolete items except at very big discounts. In the early 1980s the computer industry worked with an average 7 year product life, which was reduced to 18 months in the early 1990s and to weeks now! By the time a product is launched the technology can be obsolete, so a company suddenly finds it can't compete or pay suppliers, one of which might be you.

Good credit control means:

1) Not giving credit to habitual late payers or risky companies.
2) Setting a maximum amount of credit based on expected volume of business and risk.
3) Assessing when is the moment to cut off credit either because of late payment or increased perceived risk.

Late payers can cause cash flow problems, especially when you have low margins, short credit periods with suppliers, high labor expenses or a mixture of these factors. On the other hand staff, tax authorities, banks and suppliers expect to be paid on time regardless of your collection problems and are often quick to take action.

The more you know about your customers and their industry the better and it is vital that this information is part of the credit check. It can't be just left up to the finance department to use old data from a credit rating agency. Input is also needed from Sales who should visit the potential customer to ensure they are a real company with adequate premises. References may be needed and you should ask around to find out if they have a good or bad payment history with other suppliers.

Many business owners are of the opinion that nowadays it is still worth serving a customer who habitually pays late to keep selling. This is clearly a decision for the top management because delayed payments cost money plus the increased risk of the slow payment turning into a bad debt. Then there would not only be the loss of profit but the cost of the goods or services, delivery costs etc.

Clear policies and procedures on setting and increasing credit limits along with a method of putting credit holds in place are essential. Any exception to normal procedures has to be authorized at the highest level or Sales (under pressure to meet their targets) may try to push the sale anyway. Sales commissions should only be paid after collection to ensure salesmen's understanding and cooperation.

Decisions to take legal action to recover debts will depend on the amount, whether you or the customer will pay the legal costs and the time and energy you will expend. Having a contract with the customer may reduce legal fees or facilitate recovering these additional costs. However, if you delay too long before taking action there may be nothing left that you can recover.

85 Forecasting Cash Needs

A Cash Flow projection is essential as part of the budget process to identify in advance whether the business will have enough funds to operate, as well as purchase new assets included in the budget.

A forecast needs to be made on a regular basis for the following weeks or months to try to avoid problems and to make the best use of any surplus cash and bank funding. Be conservative about the dates you expect your customers to pay. It's better to expect slow payment and be pleasantly surprised. It is wise, if possible, to have a contingency reserve to cover unexpected expenses or a sudden shortfall in receipts.

If for some reason you cannot make a payment when agreed with a Supplier inform them immediately. The earlier you do it the easier it will be to negotiate an extension on the payment. The same principle applies for banks. It is preferable to renegotiate deadlines before the fact than going to them when you are desperate. You have more leverage asking for a credit line if you have a reasonable balance. Get the right sort of funding; an overdraft facility if it will be a very short term need or a loan if it will be for longer.

Cash flow can vary considerably during a month and during the course of the year, not just because of seasonality. The fluctuations will increase depending on the type of business, holiday pay, bonuses, frequency of loan repayments (if any), tax and exceptional purchases. While the budget and cash flow projection for the year may have looked good, during the month there might be occasional shortages of funds. If you have a lot of small customers then cash received should be spread out. However, if you have a few large customers, inflows will be more erratic since they will probably pay on set days.

It is useful to try 'what if' scenarios to see what will happen to your Cash Flow if sales are 20 or 30% lower than forecast or a major client delays payment.

If terms with suppliers are shorter than for clients there will be a need for more working capital as the business grows. This will require greater treasury control to ensure interest charges are minimized and there are no credit incidents that might make future borrowing more expensive. Failing to pay tax on time can result in penalties as well as interest plus stress and time wasted.

A simple spread sheet can be used to project when amounts should be received and payments made for each month with the closing cash balance being the opening balance for the next month. The actual figures are then input and projections can be revised. Whilst a cash flow forecast will help identify funding problems and potential collection issues remember it is not of any use in relation to the profitability of your business.

Main Takeaways:

1.

2.

3.

Improvements to implement:

Action 1.

By: Start Date: Ready by:

Action 2.

By: Start Date: Ready by:

Action 3.

By: Start Date: Ready by:

Purchasing/Supply Chain/Procurement

The Purchasing dept. has been renamed and redefined numerous times through the 80's and 90's, but still tends to be the last function that is formally set up as a business grows. Perception about this function has been changing and in most organizations management understands that it can contribute to the top line as well as to the bottom line.

Purchasing has also increase in importance in the economic downturn.

Just to clarify the terms, Purchasing basically refers to the acquisition of goods and services while Procurement extends the scope to include expediting, supplier quality and logistics. Supply Chain Management, however, has a greater emphasis on working with both suppliers and clients to maximize efficiency. We will use the term 'Purchasing' in a broad sense for simplicity.

In **www.BusinessGrowthLevers.com/resources** you will find some tips and tools to assist you with your Purchasing.

86 Leveraging Purchasing

Purchasing departments in all businesses and industries need to establish and maintain profitable Supplier relationships. This can be a challenge due to the problem of price increases, market instability and the need to ensure supply quality.

Purchasing can't just be delegated to a secretary or a spare admin person. It needs experience and a skill set to be developed and staff with some unique characteristics to really add value to the business. Soft skills are important as buyers increasingly need to deal with Suppliers and influence colleagues outside the procurement function.

Purchasing staff need to be persistent, analytical and thorough because it is not always easy to research potential suppliers in the market and make comparisons between competing products. They also need to have a good understanding of markets and the specificities of what they are buying, plus the negotiation skills so they can get the right deal, not just the cheapest.

Business knowledge is another essential, especially an understanding its goals and values. Being able to relate to suppliers and understand their business as well is critical to getting a win-win deal. Experience in other areas such as Sales, Operations and Finance can be of benefit.

Compliance to policies is a must. If buyers don't bother getting 3 quotes or using the preferred vendors, things can quickly get out of hand. The ethical standards must be high as there are many ways a Supplier can try to gain influence such as ball game tickets and trips. As no money changes hands these are usually not looked on as bribes.

Legal knowledge is advantageous, being able to understand terms and read contracts is occasionally necessary and there is not always time (or money) to get a lawyer's opinion. If the Supplier has prepared the contract being able to spot any 'onerous' clause that is against the best interests of the company is important. Agreements need to be monitored to ensure there is compliance.

Creativity is another attribute that can be an asset in some circumstances. It may not always be easy to find the right materials or products and there could be alternative solutions. This can be the case where there is a disruption to supply, e.g. the Iceland volcanic eruptions in April 2010 halted airfreight over Europe for 6 days.

Natural disasters are frequent in some parts of the world. Plans have to be made to counter the potential effects of hurricanes, floods, earthquakes, tsunamis, fires and blizzards. This is not just the risks in your area but also suppliers' and customer locations and shipment routes in between. It is important to be able to make quick assessments of the situations, have contingency plans and alternative suppliers and transport ready if the risk, cost of disruption, or both, are high.

Purchasing departments need to focus on solutions instead of just thinking in terms of products. In emergency situations as well as on a day to day basis they should continuously ask themselves: "Are the products bought the best solution for the need that has to be filled?"

87 Improving Relationships with Suppliers

Suppliers know a great deal about your business competitors, new product developments, new technology and alternative solutions. They are in a privileged position to identify new markets and potential clients for you. It is worth getting to know them and possibly referring them to other companies so that your business may get some referrals too.

If you don't know suppliers personally and don't have regular meetings with them you will be missing an important source of information. Improving collaboration and mutual assistance is needed to set the basis for a working relationship with respect and no surprises.

Purchasers should establish high standard objectives to guide them in the supplier selection process and hold suppliers accountable for performance and delivery levels. It is important that they maintain open and professional relationship with the vendors at all times.

Some businesses do not attach much value to the type of relationship that is maintained with suppliers, so depending upon the personality of the purchaser it could be adversarial, over friendly or nonexistent.

Confrontations over prices and quality can easily sour relations if not handled diplomatically. Wasting time fighting over details, that should have been set out in written agreements, can get petty with failure to return phone calls or give prior notice of delivery changes. On the other hand if the connection is too personal, e.g. too many free lunches at the golf club, getting a fair deal could be compromised.

Supplier score cards are a way to monitor quality, service and price performance so that the best suppliers can be identified. It then becomes easy to prepare a list of preferred suppliers, ideally splitting purchases between two, thus leveraging an even better relationship through a higher volume. Suppliers should be informed of their scorecard results, in the course of the regular meetings with them as a basis for helping them increase their customer satisfaction.

Within the framework of improving relationships, discussions should occur as to how best to order, package and deliver the products to reduce costs and increase quality and efficiency for both sides. Understanding each other's business and goals goes a long way. Once trust has been earned, vendors can be involved earlier on in product design to give their input to maximize quality and minimize costs.

Eventually, after the relationship has matured, they could be potential joint venture partners, to compete for larger orders than you could handle on your own.

Nothing stays the same - staff and goals change, so keep Supplier Score Cards up to date, remember to take them to the next meeting with the supplier and review the list of Preferred Suppliers periodically.

88 Not Enough Suppliers

A potential risk occurs when the specificity of the product or service your business requires narrows down the possible suppliers to one or two. It is difficult to deal with vendors that know they are the purchaser's sole source. This potentially costly situation can be defused by developing a closer professional relationship with the supplier where both companies' interests are openly discussed and full cooperation is established.

Purchasing from only one key supplier is an even bigger risk if their business is significantly larger than yours. Extra care should be put in the planning to avoid surprises. Production schedules and forecasts need to be discussed and blanket orders placed to avoid future shortages. The Supplier Score Card for this supplier should be closely monitored because your business is at their mercy.

Depending on the size and structure of their business they may be in a position to dictate prices, terms and conditions or cut your business off if they get an order from a more important customer. Additionally, if they sneeze you might catch a cold - if something goes wrong with their business, you will suffer the consequences.

If changing is not an option, your business either has to live with this dominant supplier or look for more radical alternatives like adding a different product line. For example most filling (gas) stations now sell many non-automobile related items so that they depend less on fuel sales and leverage their location and customer base.

The Purchasing department should do everything in their power to find alternative solutions by working together with the end user department for the product or service. An adjustment in your business operations may open up other options for similar products or services.

If the Purchasing department manages to find an alternative supplier there could be reprisals if your business buys less from the key supplier. Make sure the risks of disruption in your business are minimized.

Splitting purchases between two suppliers may result in some loss of volume discounts but will bring benefits if one of the suppliers has a problem. Industrial disputes, bad weather, international conflicts and other disasters can disrupt production and deliveries. For parts or materials that are critical it is imperative to have a backup supplier who you regularly give some business to safeguard production.

While anti-monopoly rules and state controlled prices exist in a lot of countries, very often there is quite a high cost of switching between utilities like electricity and gas for heating. Public utilities can be very difficult organizations to deal with. Owning your premises and using alternative energies, particularly solar and wind, can free you to some extent but price hikes cannot be totally avoided.

If you can't get the quantity or quality that you need at a fair price then you might need to explore the possibilities for producing the item yourself. Licenses to manufacturing or a joint venture agreement are other possible options. Ponder all factors – cost, risk of doing it and not doing it, market trends, etc. and build as many scenarios as possible with the input with all departments involved.

The Purchasing department should also explore the cost of produce vs. buy (or outsource) for many aspects of the business including their own services. Market knowledge and experience with certain suppliers can bring lower costs and save headcount, training and office space. Even some large corporations outsource part of their Procurement to take advantage of external structures, expertise and access to worldwide suppliers, hence removing the dependence on one local vendor.

89 Improving Inventory Management

There are 4 main types of inventory - raw materials, work in progress finished goods and spare parts. Not all businesses carry inventory but, for those who do, efficient Inventory Management is crucial.

Failure to manage inventory properly can drain a company of cash and drive up operating costs. Additionally, inventory inaccuracies can negatively impact service levels. None of these situations is good for the long-term interests of any business! Although in accounting terms inventory is an asset it is important to keep its value at a minimum. High inventory turnover is usually linked to better profits.

The most common causes for poor Inventory control are bad planning (e.g. ignoring seasonality) which can lead to over or under-stocking, using inadequate inventory management software and systems, over-purchasing to benefit from discounts or special offers, and failing to do periodical inventory counts and reconciliations to the records.

Excess stock means that money has been spent on items that are not yet needed, which might be deteriorating and are taking up warehouse space. Inventory Turn is a term for measuring the average rate of replacement of stock. The higher the figure, the quicker items are coming in and then being sent out to customers. This is particularly important for perishable goods and in fast changing industries.

If items are clearly identified and the space is well organized then the oldest stock can be used first. Bad lighting, lack of cleaning and inadequate storage make the physical picking of items more difficult, increasing the risk of mistakes and items becoming lost. Obsolete items can often be found in the darkest corners.

A Stock Out is when there is a shortage of materials, finished goods or spare parts. This may result from keeping too low an inventory or not establishing minimum reorder levels. Running out of raw materials usually results in lost production while a shortage of finished goods or spare parts can cause lost sales, reduced customer satisfaction or both.

Having the right computer software and staff properly trained to take advantage of all the features, particularly finely tuned minimum reorder levels, will go a long way to keep costs and write-offs under control.

Warehousing or Logistics is often undervalued as a function so there is a tendency to recruit poorly qualified staff, pay badly and not bother to train them adequately. The result can be lack of knowledge, skills, motivation and increased risk of theft. There is far more to the job than driving a forklift.

To ensure Inventory problems don't put the business at risk there need to be written policies and procedures with clear responsibilities for each task. There must also be thorough investigation of discrepancies between the quantities on the computer and those found in the warehouse. Additionally there must be tight control over slow-moving items along with production shortages and costly overnight shipments.

Urgent steps must be taken to get Inventory Management under control, including studying the strategies that affect inventory, reviewing and adjusting the forecasting systems, the purchasing and ordering policies, the accuracy of the data used to make the ordering decisions and the information flow and physical control of deliveries.

Working closely with suppliers to establish the optimum reorder levels and reduce delivery times is essential for a well-managed inventory. Set up automated systems to track stock and ensure that appropriate inventory counts and reconciliations exist to avoid surprises. Adapt the processing environment to inventory replenishment needs and implement a financial reconciliation process that ensures that slow moving inventories do not present an obsolescence risk. Assign ongoing responsibility and performance measurements in each area.

Inventory management is more than just about stock levels. Focus on the factors that affect the inventory and all its implications across Sales, Production, Maintenance, quality, Finance and Customer Satisfaction and your business will be more successful.

90 Reducing Waste and Inefficiency

Unfortunately sometimes Purchasing departments only get attention when there is a recession or the business gets into some sort of trouble. Far more importance is placed on Sales, Operations and Finance even though Purchasing can present opportunities for major savings that can be used to finance healthy growth.

Many companies view inventory costs as a necessity for doing business. The whole impact on costs though is significantly higher and includes holding costs (warehousing, theft, damage, insurance, physical inventory counting), obsolescence, opportunity costs (missed sales due to lack of stock) or sales returns (due to product deterioration).

Standardization is the logical starting point that enables the ordering and receiving processes to be systematized. If properly negotiated, annual contracts can be made with preferential suppliers. Mutual knowledge of strategy and systems can help shape a win-win relationship by adjusting the procedures to benefit both parties. This will help drive costs down, since better conditions can be achieved such as volume discounts, fixed prices and extended payment terms.

A Just-in-Time strategy is a subsequent step that reduces raw material and in-process inventory. However implementation requires more than a tune-up of the inventory management system. The forecasting, ordering and receiving all have to be integrated into one process so the right material is where it needs to be at the right time. Cross functional teamwork is vital for success since shortages that disrupt production and sales can cost more than savings from lower stock levels.

Quality control is a further area where waste can be avoided and hence savings made. It needs to start with the raw materials from suppliers being rigorously controlled to ensure nothing is used that may cause a problem with an end customer. It always works out cheaper in the long run to avoid a problem than to have to fix it afterwards.

The cost of shipping and handling a faulty product can exceed the profit and often it is less expensive to substitute than to repair. Specifications set out clearly in the order, or preferably the contract, have to be insisted upon with vendors. Quality certification is a prerequisite for the automobile and aviation industries where minute variations in component specs can have disastrous consequences.

Finally, internal controls with segregation of duties are imperative unless values at stake are low. This entails having different people approve purchases, receive ordered materials, approve invoices for payment, review and reconcile financial records and perform inventory counts. If duties are not separated the potential consequences are unauthorized or unnecessary purchases, excessive costs incurred, theft and goods purchased for personal use. However as with any other system throughout the organization, a cost / benefit analysis should be performed and repeated periodically to determine the adequate level of systems and controls that would optimize the supply chain.

This evaluation should be carried out by people from different departments using input from the main suppliers and the support of Finance. The goal is to simplify processes and make them more efficient, decrease waste and activities that do not add value so that profits can be maximized without risking operations or the quality of products or services.

Main Takeaways:

1.

2.

3.

Improvements to implement:

Action 1.

By: Start Date: Ready by:

Action 2.

By: Start Date: Ready by:

Action 3.

By: Start Date: Ready by:

IT

Information Technology plays an integral part in all walks of life in modern society. When computers first started to be used by businesses there were concerns by labor and trade unions that they would reduce the number of jobs. However quite the opposite has occurred, with many new occupations being created.

Over a short period of time - less than twenty years - we have come to be highly dependent on IT. Unfortunately there is the ever present risk of systems failing due to various types of attacks and electrical problems. Although back-ups and system security have steadily improved over the years there is still considerable vulnerability. Few companies have adequate emergency plans or hard-copy backups so they could continue to do business if they had no computer systems.

In **www.BusinessGrowthLevers.com/resources you** will find some tips to assist you with IT.

91 Overcoming Fear of IT

The term 'IT' or 'Information Technology' has been in use since 1958 when it was first defined in an article published in the Harvard Business Review but it still confuses a lot of people. IT is now regarded as comprising computers, peripheral hardware (printers, external disks etc.), software and telecom network links.

Information technology is a phenomenon that has dramatically changed the daily lives of individuals and businesses throughout the world. One of the key aspects for the success of a business nowadays is to be able to leverage information technology for internal systems and to communicate with the world. Information technology assists organizations to work more efficiently and to maximize productivity.

The biggest hindrance to implementing new technology doesn't usually lay in the particularities of the technology itself or even the investment (which has reduced over time). It usually comes from people and their fear. Fear of change is part of human nature and if technology isn't chosen and installed with this reality in consideration implementation will be much more difficult and training less effective. Additionally, people using the system will take too long to buy-in to its advantages whether they are aware or not that their fear is getting in the way.

Businesses need to select a technology that meets their needs and improves the efficiency of operations, but they also need to be prepared to support the staff in coping with the changes that technology is going to bring. If the end users and managers are involved in the process from the beginning, helping to define the needs and providing input, they will feel part of the change process and they will be more inclined to make implementation a success.

Another factor that creates fear is the number of new words that have come into everyday use because of IT. There are a lot of English terms used in non-English speaking countries plus acronyms, abbreviations or 'made up' terms. 'Techies' have become like a tribe and the use of techno-babble may put non-techie people off. It is important to make sure that people understand what they are expected to do and that both in training and in the interactions between IT and the users there is an effort to make sure that everything is clear and understood. People don't like to admit they don't know something because of appearing to be ignorant or stupid, so they may avoid reporting issues and just try to conceal any mistakes or problems.

Despite computers becoming a commodity that is more intuitive and user-friendly, there is still some distrust of them. Businesses are very vulnerable to loss of data, either through users' negligence or as a result of viruses or hackers. Software can be expensive, have compatibility problems, poor instruction manuals, require frequent updates and extensive time to learn to use effectively.

Decide which software is most critical for the business and take some time to get familiar with how it is used. For example see how web pages can be updated and altered by sitting with the people making the changes and asking questions. They, in turn, may have some suggestions that could improve the web site although web pages are not always easy to change and text can't be any size, font or color.

Once people start taking an interest and reading about IT, even if it is for entertainment, their 'techie quotient' goes up and understanding of technology issues becomes gradually better. The good news is that with video tutorials, remote assistance and the end users increasing literacy everything is becoming easier and easier…

92 Lack of Solutions

Is your company built around your computer system or your computer system built to support your company?

Every business, from small sole proprietorships to large conglomerates, has information-technology needs. IT and IS managers and consultants are responsible for translating executive and departmental business goals into a technology plan, ensuring the solutions align with existing best practices. Building the right technological infrastructure for any business has a large impact on its efficiency and bottom line.

The most common areas where smaller businesses need IT solutions (in-house or outsourced) are:

Accounting Systems - without the right software the financial information input is slow and arduous. Reliable data will not be available quickly to assist management. Most new packages allow faster input and access to all of the information needed to make informed financial decisions plus the flexibility to easily create different reports and calculate financial ratios at any time.

Inventory Management - accounting systems can help you track inventory costs and profitability per item, but additional systems are needed to track shipments and actually 'manage' stock. The process can be improved by the use of bar codes and automating purchase orders (generated when quantities fall below a pre-determined amount). If the business has a sales force out visiting clients using mobile devices they will be able to see what is available in real time and place orders that affect inventory immediately, thus serving clients better.

Communication - in many companies, email is the principal means of communication between employees, suppliers and customers (it's quick and avoids misunderstandings because things are 'in writing'). If the organization has multiple locations staff can communicate using VOIP telephones (Voice Over Internet Protocol), video-conferencing and live chat systems. Internet makes life easier for small-businesses by allowing them to interact with prospects and clients in their Website or Social Media page, research suppliers, job applicants and strategic partners.

Data Management and Security - most organizations keep digital versions of documents and store the physical documents elsewhere cheaper and safer. Digital documents can be instantly available to everyone who is authorized to see them (additional protection) regardless of where they are located, saving time and photocopies.

Customer Relationship Management (CRM) - IT allows improvement of customer relationships by tracking every interaction a company has with each customer. This is an efficient and less time consuming process and the business can provide a better, more personalized experience to each client.

Software suppliers have come a long way in recognizing customers' needs. Modular solutions provided flexible systems that could easily be integrated. More recently the offerings have changed to layered products where solutions for small businesses can be upgraded to medium size without redesigning documents, data bases and work flows. Cloud based solutions also enhance flexibility with access from any location with internet. Cloud based is cost effective since usually the monthly fee is per user and the supplier has full responsibility for performance, updates and upgrades, backups and maintenance. Risk is also reduced since the service providers should be in a better position to protect data from hackers and viruses than small companies.

93 Improving Implementation

When planning the implementation of an IT solution, experts and business managers should build a plan based on the most cost effective technological solution. They have to consider the impact the change will have on the business and the risk of negative consequences in the quality of the product or service. Conducting business as usual while learning, training and migrating to a new system is hard. Transition has to be planned so that impact on production and clients is minimized.

Most systems' implementations take longer than expected because of resistance to change but also to ensure that quality standards are not affected. During most implementation processes employees are asked to tend to the tasks of their core job and contribute to the software project. The main reason is to keep costs under control but it is also to have their knowledge of the day to day operations.

A big challenge that transitioning software solutions poses is migrating the data while keeping operations running. Weekends are ideal but sometimes not enough. If either outside consultants or the software house is running the process, the contract should contemplate adequate compensation in case of loss of data, unforeseen system downtime, etc.

The frustration of systems working slowly, crashing or failing to work completely has reduced with hardware and software becoming faster and more robust and solutions more standardized and flexible. Being locked into a certain technology or supplier was a major problem in the past and lack of adequate solutions or exorbitant prices could hinder the growth of the business. Linux and other open source software have gone a long way to overcoming these drawbacks.

Everything needs to be planned to exhaustion considering different scenarios where things could go wrong and damage controlled. In any case it is good practice to keep both systems running – the old and the new – so that outputs can be compared and the differences analyzed until everything is running smoothly.

Even with planning, many things can go wrong during the implementation process. It is important to set up a plan that is the result of consensus between management, IT experts and users. This plan should include clear goals, milestones to be met along the way and deadlines. A careful audit of each milestone will help you ensure that the team or the service providers are on track.

Any major deviation from what was planned has to result in focused action from all the parties involved so that problems are pinpointed as early as possible in the project's lifecycle to avoid downstream impacts.

The project leader should have the authority and ability to make decisions along the way in order to course correct and keep the process moving. Failure to progress on the project is guaranteed to lengthen the implementation time and increase costs.

94 Lack of Training

Lack of a well-planned, detailed, comprehensive and tailored training program to be run during all the phases of the implementation process can be a major setback for any software project.

Let's assume a new IT solution was being implemented throughout the company. Different people will have different training needs. Managers need more focus on analysis and decision-making features while staff need to learn a new way to do their jobs. However all users need training in the basics to understand the benefits and how all the pieces fit together. It is important to picture how an action by an employee – let's say receiving a shipment - triggers a serious of events throughout the organization (stock increases in Inventory and in Accounting and updated information in the sales force mobile devices). Managers will gain a better understanding of how the staff will be performing and which additional information the system will be able to provide.

When the staff does not understand what the new system is supposed to do and how to operate it, they will not be motivated to learn and are likely to use it incorrectly, which can lead to a longer implementation period. The same problem occurs if training is not well planned and is inconsistent or inadequate.

General information on the system should be provided before implementation starts. Traditional classroom training complemented with further reading is usually the best approach. As implementation starts and progresses, training will be on the job and customized to each department or even to each person or group that performs exactly the same task.

Trainers, management and staff need to work together to address issues that may come up and find solutions so the milestones defined for the implementation process are achieved. Embedded learning, training modules built into the product or equipment, will help users to learn and support them when the trainer is not there.

Tutorials are especially helpful for standard software used throughout the organization (Word, Excel, etc.) but can be challenging and confusing because they were designed to do a lot more than most users need. There are plenty of one day courses available to learn the basics for these tools, but it is helpful to have a mentor within the organization to assist in the practical specific needs.

Having an IT 'expert' who can sit beside the staff and look over their shoulder for 30 minutes is not a good solution. Chances are that during that time they will be interrupted or will be texting or troubleshooting another installation. Nothing beats dedicated training, without interruptions, where a comprehensive understanding of the software is achieved, not just the normal small part that will be used day-to-day. Saving money on training is not a smart move as it can compromise the whole investment made in the system.

Your software provider needs to have an ongoing education program like webinars, online product documentation or new feature training sessions plus an efficient help desk. What happens if a new member of staff is hired or someone needs to brush up their skills in a certain area? You cannot rely on them just being coached by an experienced user. The person may not have the time or skills to explain everything or be working in the most efficient way themselves. It is important that all users and systems perform at their best.

95 Information Overload

The implementation of IT solutions has allowed most businesses to have the ability to capture data from customer transactions and day-to-day operations and make thorough research. If before the problem was not having enough information about prospects and clients, nowadays the challenge is what to do with all the accumulated data and how to turn it into intelligence that can improve the bottom line. This also applies to other areas of the business.

When is information too much information? Is it really worthwhile having the systems to gather so much data if it means 'wasting' a lot of time analyzing it and preparing reports that nobody really looks at or cares about?

The answer in theory is simple. All information that can be processed and used to improve relationships with clients and prospects, the quality of products and services, the control and efficiency of operations and to support strategic management decisions to improve the bottom line is needed.

In real life businesses have to battle with limited resources, principally money and staff. It is important for each business to find the sweet spot that allows the best combination of financial and quality control with the best service to the client taking into consideration the resources available.

It is not so much the quantity of information but what you do with it. There seldom is a "silver bullet" that resolves all problems, so the key issues need to be identified and quantified. With limited resources for managing or improving systems it is difficult to change practices and processes as staff often resist if they can't see the long term gain, especially if they have to put time and effort to learn a new system.

Quick fixes may not give the best long term gains but may help getting traction for changes to stick. This would apply for modular software or systems that have a simplified version that could be used to 'test the waters'. Cloud based solutions where staff access the software as needed paying for access, time logged on, number of transactions processed, storage used, or a combination can be an alternative although the downside is a lack of control.

Some people associate information overload with a lot of files and reports piled up on a desk. IT solutions make it possible for organizations to have an almost paperless work environment. Besides being ecological, this reduces the feeling of overwhelm and allows for data to me presented in a more visual way – namely through charts and diagrams. If prepared automatically by the system this frees up additional time for better analysis.

To select the right IT solution for the business it is wise to use a bottom up approach whereby users are consulted and involved. If planned correctly, the new system will be able to process the information to allow greater management control and make it accessible from any computer or mobile device, enabling staff to perform more effectively and efficiently. Additionally, with more accurate data available for projections, management can make more realistic long-term strategic plans.

Making the best use of information solutions and resources available in the organization will improve operational efficiency and profitability.

96 Evaluating the ROI

The Return on Investment (ROI) ratio is a good tool for evaluating investment decisions and it is only natural to try to apply it to purchasing software or IT solutions. One of the formulas used is:

ROI=(gain from investment–cost of investment)/(cost of investment)

The ROI of a project should only play a small part in the decision process due to its limitations – it is a financial ratio that does not take into consideration the intangible benefits to the organization. In most cases ROI is used as a tool to predict and then review actual results of investment on IT solutions implementations. The actual ROI is normally higher because of the impact of qualitative factors.

Like any other change in an organization, an IT solution is an investment for which the benefits should exceed the amount spent. In many cases though, more important than detailed ROI calculations, is to know if the return is going to be positive, breakeven, or negative.

Technological evolution is not really an option. The issue is the extent of the investment to be made. The use of metrics such of ROI with pre-determined and uniform criteria will allow comparison between solutions and provide support for management and IT experts to decide which solution/supplier to select. The same process can be used to prioritize different phases that cannot be implemented simultaneously due to timing and resource constraints.

Some organizations find it relatively easy to measure the cost or investment but most have trouble measuring benefits. A simplified way of calculating increased revenue resulting from the investment is merely looking at the sales before and after, which is adequate in some situations. With IT implementation processes most of the benefits come from increased efficiency that results in cost reductions and improved customer satisfaction.

Some savings can be easy to measure like reduced paper costs and decreased personnel needs while others are more difficult to quantify like increased productivity. Other benefits include increased job satisfaction and motivation, more timely information for management, competitive advantages with customers by decreasing response time and increasing quality of service and finally better corporate image.

As to investment and costs the most significant will be on equipment, software, wiring or other work needed on the premises, manpower – consultants, new staff plus staff overtime and training. However, costs also involve other resources such as office space, travel and opportunity cost of the staff that could be doing other tasks or will lose productivity or underperform in their current task.

An efficient way to review the benefits is to ask each department what would be the cost of not having the proposed new IT solution.

An efficient IT system can change the entire culture of an organization.

A long term benefit is the organizational flexibility and transparency and the fact that the business has a system that is integrated and will support growth in a more efficient and cost effective way.

Main Takeaways:

1.

2.

3.

Improvements to implement:

Action 1.

By: Start Date: Ready by:

Action 2.

By: Start Date: Ready by:

Action 3.

By: Start Date: Ready by:

Miscellaneous

97 Finding the Right Partners

At first glance, taking on a partner seems like a great idea. It can be both stimulating and reassuring to have partners who share the same dream and values as you. The reasons are simple: combining forces with others that have complementary skill sets and can help with the tough decisions, to share equipment or expenses, and often provide a cash inflow to leverage the intellectual capital.

Unfortunately, the fact is that partnerships, like marriages, have less than a 50% chance of surviving in the long term. However, most failures could have been avoided with smarter planning upfront.

Future partners should make sure they share a common vision for both the business and the partnership. It is important this vision is put in writing and revisited frequently to ensure partners are still in alignment.

Each partner should have a clear understanding of why they and the other(s) are in the partnership. This helps define roles, responsibilities and expectations, and can lead to constructive discussion as things evolve over time. Partnering with someone because you can't afford to hire them is a partnership killer because there will be a perceived disparity between contribution and reward and perception is reality.

It is also important that each partner is aware of their own strengths and weaknesses as well as those of their partners. Usually there is a general idea of who will do what based on their skills and preferences. It is vital to lay out clearly each person's roles and responsibilities beforehand, have basic systems and procedures in writing and introduce a formal method for making decisions and addressing disagreements. In more difficult situations, you can also turn to an advisory board or a consultant for help.

The need for power and to be the dominant partner ruins many businesses. Egos are hard to hold in check when there is success and this can compromise future success. Job titles can become an issue and the united front that made the business strong can be hurt by turf wars.

Disagreement over money is an early sign of a partnership headed for a crisis. One partner wants to take more money out of the business and the other wants to reinvest. Unless the reason is a health or family issue it shows different long term strategies and this can compromise the company's growth and even the financial stability.

Some people believe family businesses are stronger because of blood ties; others consider working with family is hard and compromises creativity. Of course it all depends on the character of the individuals, since family and business can be a complex mix.

Have a lawyer create a clear business agreement upfront, even if it is short and simple. This may seem obvious but often doesn't happen to avoid the cost. In most cases it will be an expensive mistake. The agreement should include the roles and responsibilities, compensation structure, etc. but most importantly address the issue of how to exit - what will happen to the business if a partner wants to leave.

A business doesn't have to close if the partners decide to part ways. It is unfair to the staff, clients and other stakeholders. If a compromise cannot be reached, having a pre-agreed valuation method for a partner to leave will avoid a lot of pain and allow the company to keep going.

98 Succession

Grooming a person to take control in the future or even preparing someone to manage the day to day while you take a well-earned vacation is essential for the continuity of the business. Your employees depend on you and if you don't ensure that business will continue without you then you are putting their income at risk.

In an ideal world the best employees, who demonstrate leadership qualities, would be the ones who reach the top. In reality, the practice of favoring and promoting relatives or protégés is widely practiced, independently of the size of the company.

Lack of recognition is one of the most common reasons why people leave their jobs. Perceived favoritism will cause dissatisfaction among the staff and lower productivity and morale. There will be less incentive for high performance if staff feels that the path to promotion is undermined by nepotism.

On the other hand, if the employees who are rewarded and promoted are not the best qualified or fit to the job this can lead to a decrease in the level of performance and efficiency, weak leadership and further demoralization of more deserving candidates.

Many companies include anti-nepotism (and anti-fraternization) policies in their employee handbook. Some prohibit the hiring of an employee's relatives, while others only prohibit it if there would be a direct or indirect reporting connection between the related individuals. The purpose is to protect the business from situations that could interfere with operations and have an impact in the bottom line.

When pre-existing personal relationships take precedence over actual qualifications in the hiring process, the adverse effects on morale are likely to be felt by all parties involved. Management may feel that staff resents the decision, question their judgment and ethics and think the decisions involving that person will always be biased. The employee may be entering the workplace under a cloud of ill-feeling. All their actions are likely to be scrutinized and judged. Staff may display hostile feelings or attempt to sabotage the new hire or, if the person is in a leadership position, they may reduce productivity.

Not all instances of nepotism are bad. It may take a while to earn the respect of the coworkers, but if the person is committed to not letting the business down the initial stigma of being the boss's son will fade over time and the work relationship will proceed as normal.

Often the family relationship is one where higher levels of trust and responsibility exist. Going the extra mile can be easier if it is for the family business than for someone else. There is also a greater knowledge of the other person such as their skills, talents and character so that working together is often easier. In addition they may be the natural person to run the enterprise when the time comes.

Managing the handover of power is not easy and needs to be well planned and carried out, especially if more than one person is in the running to take control. Stepping away from the daily management and working on the changes that need to be made for a smooth hand-over and growth of the business can give a new perspective of things. The successor can gain valuable experience while you are still there to maintain a close watch on events.

99 Innovation

"Vision without execution is hallucination"
Thomas Edison

It is easy to blame chief executives and senior management for not devoting enough attention to introducing new products, but that is a too simplistic reason for new products being rare. Successful strategic innovations need more than a great idea. Ideas are a dime a dozen and there is no shortage of new product concepts. Often, it is a recognition problem and ideas that surface in one organization and were ignored, appear later in another and turn out to be huge successes!

Ideas and product concepts by themselves are worthless. You need to move from idea to execution, which is where many companies fall short! It is important to have a new-product development process clearly laid out, efficient and repeatable, which allows your business to turn an idea into something that sells and makes a profit.

As competition for customers and resources has become more intense, the ability to innovate has evolved into a key element for the business and is often more important than any other factor in its sustainability. However innovation does not have to be the application of new technologies or the carrying out of formal research and development. Innovation is the process of seeking to gain a competitive advantage in the market place and to increasing the ability to generate wealth.

In small businesses the owner manager is often too busy running operations and keeping the company afloat. As a result, innovation often comes as a response to solving a problem or difficulty. If a product or service is no longer selling well the decision has to be made to remodel, redesign or retire. Innovation can be evolutionary, increments that make a product better or more in line with customer tastes, or revolutionary, where something new comes into existance. In both instances creativity is required and there is some risk.

The advantage of small businesses is their size which allows more dynamism, internal flexibility, shorter lead times and openness to change. The disadvantages are greater difficulty in attracting capital, not having the size to have proper R&D and the capacity to handle the large financial risk of launching a completely new product. Larger companies can find synergies with other products or partners.

Making things differently, better, quicker or more cost efficient are very important forms of innovation in small businesses. Other examples could be better methods of production, packaging and delivery that reduce costs, cut waste and increase efficiency or better products and services offered to customers, development of lean processes, new management techniques and best practices implementation.

Stimulating creativity and an atmosphere where all ideas are welcome and respected, no matter how outrageos, is not an easy task but one that could result in the next miracle product.

100 Showing Gratitude

> *"Be thankful for what you have; you'll end up having more. If you concentrate on what you don't have, you will never, ever have enough."*
> *Oprah Winfrey*

Feeling appreciated lifts people up because it makes them feel safe and energized to perform at their best. On the other hand, when people feel they are not appreciated at work they lose motivation, feel less inclined to help fellow workers or be pleasant to customers.

At work, as in life, one of the most important things for human beings is the feeling that we truly matter and that we contribute a unique value to the business, the family, the big picture. However, open praising or the expressing of appreciation is seldom practiced at work; in many organizations it is regarded as awkward, a waste of time since people are paid to perform well, right?

Heartfelt appreciation is a muscle that is not exercised in most organizations. Feedback usually comes in its negative form to let the employee know they have to improve performance.

People who approach life with a sense of gratitude are constantly aware of what is wonderful in their life. If you focus on the positive you will get more of it. By contrast, people who lack gratitude usually focus on what they do not have or on what is wrong with their lives. Consequently feel unhappier, discouraged and less likely to succeed.

In the world of business gratitude started getting noticed for showing positive results in the effect it had on clients. A simple card saying 'thank you for shopping with us' or 'we appreciate your business' built customer loyalty so gratitude became part of most interactions with customers.

So if 'thank you' works so well with customers, why not appreciation in the workplace to build a high performing, motivated team? Gratitude is not something that is passed only from the boss to the employee. To have a real positive impact in the workplace employees should show it to one another and to their bosses. Everyone can show gratitude in a workplace and influence others to do so.

If everyone makes it a priority to notice what others are doing right (and mention it) before they point out the mistakes, they will get the other person's attention first and get them in the mood to improve. We are all more vulnerable than we show or want to acknowledge and that's why there is so much stress at work. Authentically appreciating others will make you feel better about yourself too and the human habit of reciprocity will soon make the workplace a more pleasant environment that fosters growth and productivity which will eventually impact the bottom line.

101 Resilience and Persistence

Resilience is the ability to bounce back after a setback while persistence is the determination to see something through to the end. In both cases it depends on the way you see problems, either as a challenge or as the gods saying you can't do it.

The economy and the markets are evolving at unprecedented speed, faster than the pace at which many organizations have been able to adapt. Big and small businesses are failing more frequently. More bankruptcies are being filed. Corporate earnings are more erratic. Even companies that have always been successful are finding it more difficult to deliver the same returns.

It is important to have a good business model, quality, industry know-how, loyal customers, a well-known brand and physical assets, but it is no longer a guaranty for long term success. Today's success lies in continuously anticipating and having the ability to dynamically reinvent or adjust business models and strategies as circumstances change.

Organizations are more than the sum of the individuals, they are teams. However teams can only be as resilient as the people who are in them. Organizations need resilient individuals who think critically and creatively when under intense pressure from outside circumstances and control their feelings under all conditions. They need leaders who are emotionally intelligent and have learnt to be socially aware of others and to overcome their weaknesses and leverage their strengths.

Resilience and willpower allow us to learn to prioritize our time effectively and learn to make better and more effective decisions on a daily basis. By developing the resilience 'muscle' business owners, managers and staff will be able to take actions that are aligned with the organization's objectives despite the problems and setbacks that stand in the way, and regardless of the difficulties that are pulling them back to their comfort zone

Organizations need individuals with self-discipline who can direct their focus, persist and commit to a desired outcome. Clear goals and a strong sense of purpose will help staying on track. When you develop the ability to anticipate problems you can better prepare yourself for what's yet to come and look for solutions, answers and opportunities that you can take advantage of if the problems do arise.

Mistakes and setbacks are only temporary pit-stops along your journey that present you with an opportunity to learn from your experience and therefore make better and more effective decisions in the future.

> *"The person interested in success has to learn to view failure as a healthy, inevitable part of the process of getting to the top."*
> *Joyce Brothers*

Small and progressive steps daily are more effective than large steps taken occasionally and erratically. Remember momentum is created when you move forward steadily towards your goals and objectives.

> *"In essence, if we want to direct our lives, we must take control of our consistent actions. It's not what we do once in a while that shapes our lives, but what we do consistently."*
> *Tony Robbins*

You may be wondering why the book is called: **Business Growth Levers - 100 Challenges you can turn into opportunities** and there are 101.

Delivering more than is expected is one of the ways to build good customer relations. Hence an additional 'challenge' that I hope will support you in your journey to make your business grow.

Made in the USA
San Bernardino, CA
16 April 2014